Echoes of the Past. Crafting and Playing Ancient Rim-Blown Flutes: Kawala, Saluang, Ney, and the Native American Pueblo (Anasazi) Flute

For the most important people in my life, Corinne, Mariam, Noah, Tabea, Eli, and Moshira. And for those who wish to follow in the footsteps of our flute-making ancestors, who built and played rim-blown flutes with advanced scales thousands of years ago.

Marwan Hassan

Echoes of the Past.
Crafting and Playing Ancient Rim-Blown Flutes

Kawala, Saluang, Ney,
and the Native American Pueblo (Anasazi) Flute

Bibliographic Information from the German National Library:
The German National Library lists this publication in the German National Bibliography;
Detailed bibliographic data can be accessed online at dnb.dnb.de.

© 2024 Marwan Hassan

Fotos: Corinne, Mariam, Noah and Marwan Hassan
Foto of ancient Egyptian Ney Player in the Tomb of Nenkhefetka: Mai Haikal

Publisher: BoD · Books on Demand GmbH, In de Tarpen 42, 22848 Norderstedt
Printed: Libri Plureos GmbH, Friedensallee 273, 22763 Hamburg

ISBN: 978-3-7597-7685-3

Figure 1: Ney Player and Singer. A painted relief from the tomb of Nenkhefetka (approx. 2400 BC). [Photo by Mai Haikal]

Contents

A Brief Story

I was about 14 when I took a bus from Cairo to Sharm El-Sheikh. At that time, it was a ghost town with a few cheap hotels and fiberglass huts for rent. Sinai had just been returned to Egypt after the peace treaty with Israel. Most of the scattered ruins were remnants of the Israeli occupation.

From there, I went to Nuweiba for a few nights, then took a bus to Saint Catherine at Mount Moses. I fell in love with this place at first sight and kept returning for years. Around Saint Catherine, you could go on several wandering safari tours through the desert to small oases with fresh, cold water.

I used to go there with two friends, and later on, I started spending a week or two on my own on a mountain opposite Mount Moses, hearing and watching tourists' pilgrimage at dawn to catch the sunrise from the top of the mountain. My best companion was my Ney flute. I would play a tune, wait a second or two for the echo, and then play together with the echo. While writing these words, I still can hear these echoes after almost 40 years, like echoes of the past.

One day, though, I heard a sound like a Ney, but it was not a Ney. It was melancholic and had a scale I had never heard before in this voice. I followed the sound and approached two Bedouin women who started screaming when they saw me. I was young and did not know it was improper to approach Bedouin women grazing their goats in the desert. I just wanted to know which instrument they were playing. Then, a tall man came shouting at me aggressively. As I understood later, he thought I was after his daughters. Me, a tourist, in only shorts! I told the man I was a Ney player and had only followed the tune. He grabbed the flute from one of his daughters, handed it to me, and said, "Show me if you can play it."

Now, you need to know that this instrument, which turned out to be the Kawala, is played like the Ney, only with a different fingering, so it was easy for me to produce a clean sound. Only then did the Bedouin father calm down. I asked him if I could measure the flute. It was made from an old water pipe and had only four holes! I had nothing but my hands and fingers, so I measured it with them.

When I returned to Cairo, I replicated these measurements. At some point, I learned that a very similar flute is a folk instrument played at feasts in Upper Egypt with originally six holes. After some research, I found that this flute type is spread over almost the entire world. In fact, a similar flute was discovered in Germany, called the Neanderthal flute, dating back up to 50,000 years BC.

Playing this flute means connecting to humanity's most ancient wind instrument, far beyond religion, nations, and ideologies. It is the flute of all our ancestors. It is the origin of the Ney, Saluang, Native American Pueblo flute, the Shakuhachi, and many other flutes. Hence, we will start with the Kawala and gradually learn how to build some flutes I mentioned here. Whichever flute you choose from this book to learn to make or play, you will be echoing our ancestors' music, sounds, and emotions from a time long before territorial, ideological, political, or religious conflicts arose.

Introduction

In mid-2008, a talented flutist from the Munich Philharmonic commissioned me to build a Ney for the musical The Lord of the Rings. It was intended for the second flute in the piece "Gandalf's Lament" to be played with either an alto flute or Ney.

The standard Ney set consists of seven flutes, each corresponding to a specific oriental scale. All Neys have the same ratio between the hole positions and the flute's size; only the Ney's length determines the base note to which the flute is tuned. A distinctive feature of the Ney is that when the third finger hole from the bottom is opened, it always produces a quarter tone. To give you a more visual idea, imagine a keyboard.

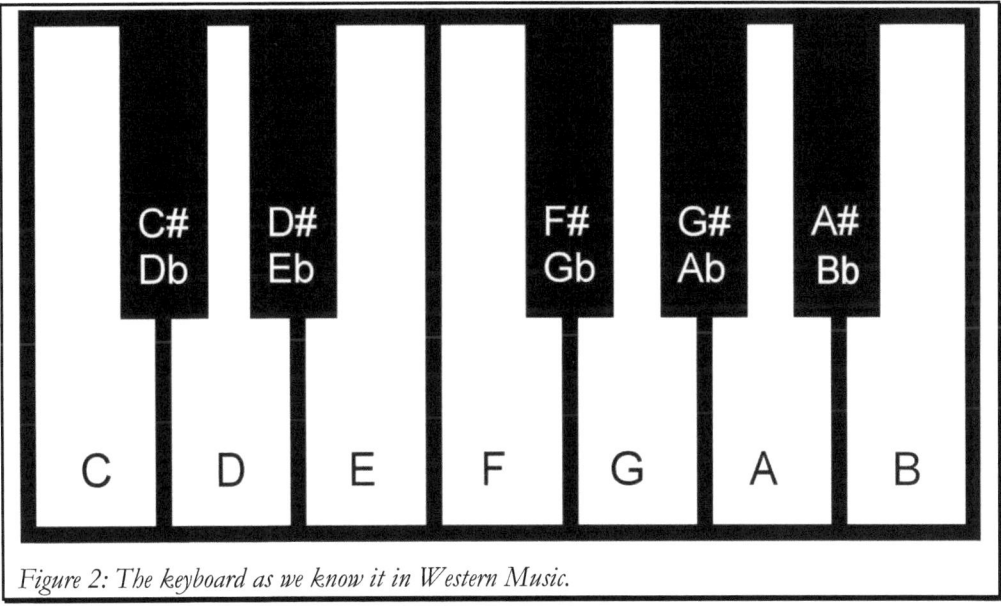

Figure 2: The keyboard as we know it in Western Music.

Western music has 12 notes from C to B, which are well-suited for creating harmonies and chords. In contrast, oriental music focuses on the perfection of the individual notes rather than on creating harmony through chords. Instead of just twelve notes, it includes 24 notes in an octave. For example, between C and C#, Arabic music adds a C ¼#. And between Eb and E, there is an E ¼b.

Those who did not grow up with these sounds need time to hear them accurately. For people from the Orient, what may be perceived as wailing by a Western ear is perfection in musical nuance.

It reminds me of a situation I encountered while living in Dubai. I was working on writing a guide for an incentive tours agency there. I

Figure 3: Left: C plus a quarter tone. Right: E minus a quarter tone.

often spent the entire night in the office because it was overcrowded and noisy during the day. After one of these long nights, I was about to print everything I had collected and written. Just then, the Bengali kitchen assistant asked, shaking his head, "A copy, Sir?"

I explained to the employee that I did not need a copy. He immediately asked again, emphasizing the word "copy." I explicitly said that I did not need a copy and that it was enough if I printed everything once! When he kept asking, I lost my temper.

The head of the travel agency looked at the situation briefly and started laughing. He comforted the assistant and took me aside. He then explained that he came from a linguistic background where he confused the letter "F" with "P." When he said "copy," he meant "coffee."

The man just wanted to offer me a coffee, and I yelled at him. I felt terrible. Apart from my apologies to him, the lesson from this story in the contest of this book is that when we have not grown up with certain sounds and tones, we cannot recognize them quickly, and it takes a while before we even begin to hear them. People tend to replace unfamiliar sounds with similar ones they are already familiar with. This also happened to me with Danish, where I kept hearing an "L" instead of the Danish "D." It is neither a "D" as we know it nor an "L," but a sound in between that can only be recognized after weeks of practice and listening.

Returning to the commission I received from the talented flutist in Munich, I was tasked with building a Ney that could play a specific Western musical piece.

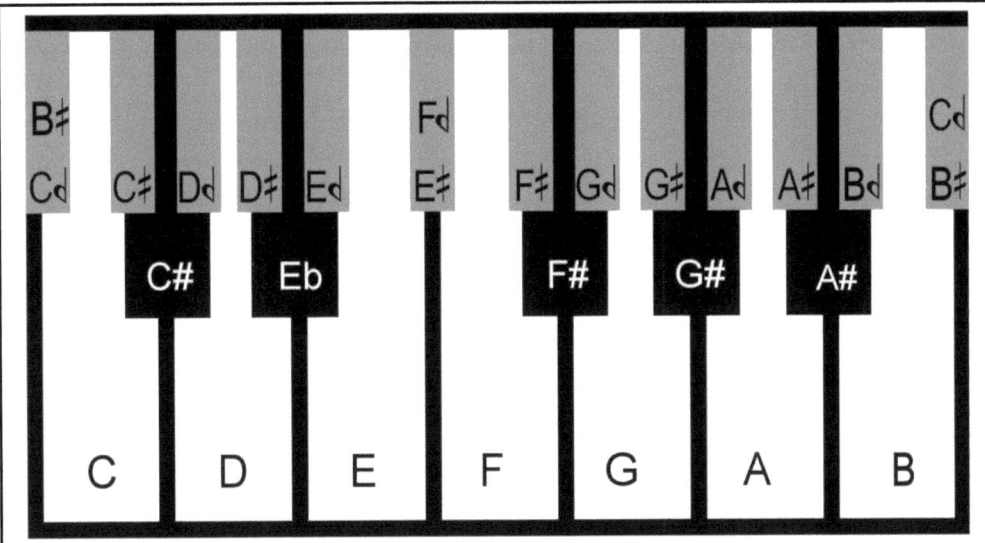

Figure 4: If there were an oriental keyboard, the quarter tones would need to be included. Here, they would be shown in grey.

Explicitly, the flute should cover the following notes: D#, F, G, G#, A, A#, C, C#, D#, E, F, F#, G#, A, and A#. The Ney most suitable for this unusual scale is the Ney Djaharka (51 cm (20.1 in) on Eb). However, I would need to close the second hole from the bottom and move the third hole about 2 cm (0.8 in) higher to achieve the fourth note expected. Furthermore, the scale would sound shrill and high. I tried to build a suitable Ney waisting three tubes, but no matter what I did, it never met the exact requirements. I almost gave up; then I remembered that Kawalas could be tuned easily arbitrarily and are, therefore, considerably more suitable for Western music, at least for this piece, than Ney flutes. I cut a bamboo tube, and within minutes, the bamboo blank for a Kawala was ready, which also met the requirements of the piece.

Years ago, I had already tried to market the Kawala in Germany. But because it is so unknown, there were only a few interested musicians. In contrast, the Ney, only conditionally suitable for Western music, is already known to many musicians and is more likely to be bought.

The Ney is an ancient Egyptian development of the older Kawala and was spread from there throughout the Orient. Strictly speaking, the Kawala (also known as Sullamiyya, Saluang, or Ghab) is the oldest wind instrument in the world, as it is merely a tube with a few holes and the prototype of the ancient Egyptian Ney, which has itself been demonstrably played for over 4000 years (See figure No. 1). Before we begin to build a Kawala, I would like to compare the Ney with the Kawala briefly.

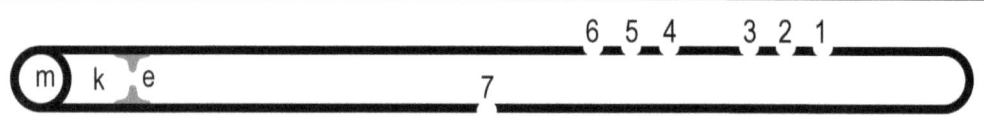

Figure 5: Directly after the mouthpiece (m), there is a chamber (k) that is about 4-5 cm (1.6-2 in) in size. The membrane (e) is pierced only about 1 cm (0.4 in) and must remain constricted. All other membranes are entirely removed. Hole No. 7 is in the middle of the flute. Under hole No. 3 lies the quarter tone. Because all the holes are located on the lower half of the flute, an Egyptian Ney can be up to 68 cm (26.8 in) long and still be easily played. The holes are close together and can, therefore, be comfortably covered. Due to the constriction (e) and the hole positions, one can play four registers on the Ney. The disadvantage: The notes can only be cleanly modulated up to a quarter tone. The advantage: Due to the chamber (k), it can easily play up to three octaves.

Although building a Ney appears simple in the figure above, the process is quite complex, considering that bamboo reeds have multiple chambers, not all membranes should be sanded away, and the hole positions must be millimeter-precise. Building a Ney is genuinely an art in itself.

Caution: Moisture can accumulate through the membrane (e), and mold is not uncommon if the interior is poorly processed and treated.

The Kawala

Its straightforward construction characterizes the Kawala. I already shared my first encounter with it in the brief story at the beginning of this book.

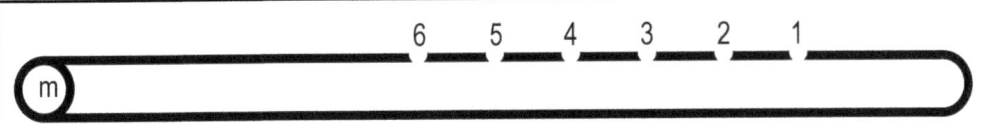

Figure 6: The Kawala has no chamber and no constriction. It is simply a tube with a sharp edge and six holes. The advantage: The Kawala is easy to clean and can be made from bamboo, wood, plastic, or an aluminum tube. The disadvantage: Since the center of the flute is below hole No. 5, Kawalas cannot be made as large as Neys. Beyond a length of 50 cm (19.7 in), it becomes difficult to reach the holes.

Just 75 years ago, in oriental music, the lute, the Ney, the qanun (oriental zither), and a few string instruments would accompany the singer, playing more or less the same melody. Since harmony and chord accompaniment have become integral parts of oriental music, and since piano, guitar, and synthesizer have become part of Arabic pop music, more and more Ney players are turning to the Kawala, which for centuries was the flute of folklore and rural areas.

Despite its major tuning, the Kawala can cover the entire spectrum of oriental music. Additionally, it can be tuned to play the typical Arabic quarter tones directly, which I will discuss at the end of the book. However, a Kawala will only offer two octaves.

The pitch can be adjusted up or down by up to half a note by slightly altering the blowing angle. Unlike the Ney, the Kawala is very sensitive to hole closing. For example, when playing the Ney, it does not matter much if you close holes 1 and 2 when holes 7, 6, and 5 are already closed. This is not the case with the Kawala.

Closing additional holes at the bottom will slightly lower the pitch, allowing for smooth transitions between notes on the Kawala.

Generally speaking, the more detailed and developed the mechanics of an instrument, the harder it is to add personal nuances between the given notes. What the lever does for the electric guitar and the pedal for the keyboard, the Kawala player achieves with their fingers and by changing the blowing angle.

The Kawala is arguably the most suitable oriental-sounding wind instrument for Western music. Of course, Kawalas and Neys cannot replace each other fully, just as a ukulele cannot replace a violin because both have four strings. However, for your introduction to oriental tones, no instrument is more suitable than the Kawala. It is also the best practice to build and play the following flutes, which we will deal with in this book.

First, I will show you in a quick guide how easy it is to build a Kawala. Then, I will guide you on improving this flute to a professional-level Kawala that can easily compete with the best in the world. In this process, you will learn extensively and in great detail how to tune bamboo flutes and treat the bamboo tube inside and out. You will learn how to make your tuning rods and shellac varnish. You will also learn how to bind your flute so that you, and potentially your customers if you choose to produce commercially, will enjoy the flute for many years.

Only after you have mastered the Kawala will we focus on further rim-blown flutes like the Saluang flutes and the Native American Pueblo flute. It is essential not only to give you template measurements for drilling the holes but also to show you how to research and recreate historical instruments yourself. Hence, I have put some special effort into showing you how to calculate the holes of the Puebloan flutes. If you study this part, you can build many historical rim-blown flutes. I strongly advise you to study the entire book. In my youth, no internet or entire book explained any of this. Nearly all I know about bamboo flutes results from decades of testing, failing, and retrying. Sure, in recent years, whenever I find a booklet or brochure on the subject, I would buy it, but I have not found any comprehensive book on this subject. Thus I decided to write it for you.

Enjoy, and good luck with building your flute(s)!

The Quick Guide to Building a Kawala

Take a tube with an inner diameter of approximately 18-20 mm (0.70-0.78 in), divide it into 12 equal sections, and drill holes at points 2, 3, 4, 5, 6, and 7, each with a diameter of about 8 - 9 mm (0.31 - 0.35 in).

That is it! You have built your first Kawala. I swear, it is really that simple. You only need a tube, a cordless drill, the appropriate drill bits, and a small sandpaper to smooth the holes after drilling.

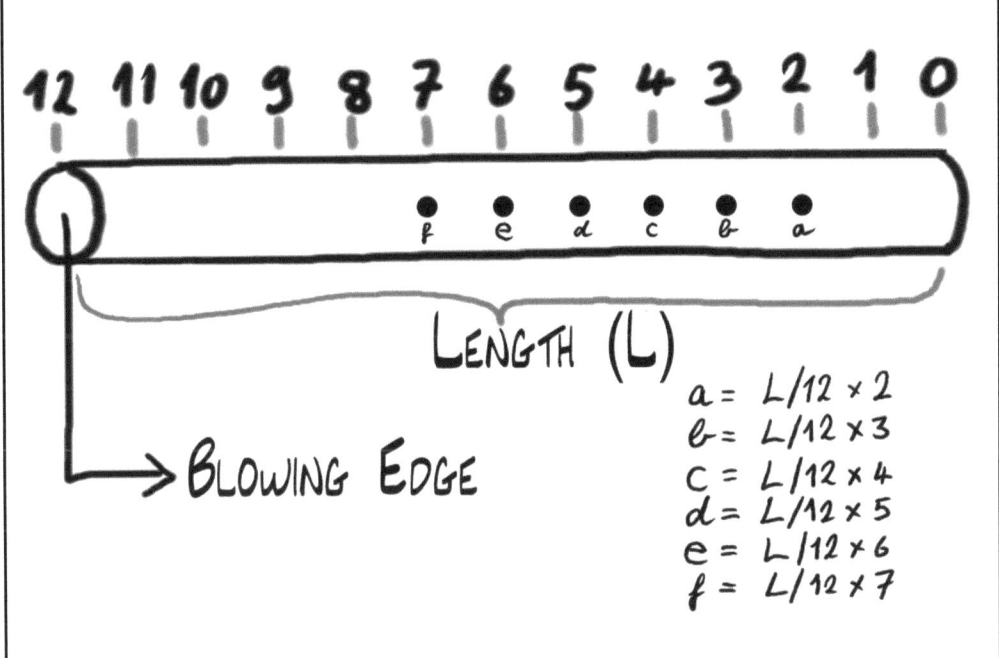

$$a = L/12 \times 2$$
$$b = L/12 \times 3$$
$$c = L/12 \times 4$$
$$d = L/12 \times 5$$
$$e = L/12 \times 6$$
$$f = L/12 \times 7$$

Figure 7: To ensure the holes are aligned, I recommend sticking a painter's masking tape along the length of the flute. Draw a line on the tape where the holes will be drilled at their respective distances. After drilling, simply remove the tape. Hold the flute at one end with one hand and wrap a piece of sandpaper around the other end. Slide the flute back and forth a few times to sand down the sharp edges created by the drilling. If necessary, you can also wrap the sandpaper around your thumb like a pointed thimble and insert it into the holes to smooth them out. **Caution**: *Beware of splinters!*

Producing the First Tone

Before building Kawala flutes, learning to produce a clean tone is essential. The Kawala is a rim-blown flute, so the sound is produced by blowing air across the edge of an open tube. Failure to play the tone correctly can result in an improperly tuned Kawala. Once you have built a Kawala using the quick guide, cover the holes with your fingers or use an aluminum or PVC pipe without holes for practice. When you can produce the correct sound, you can play music on copper pipes found in hardware stores.

Theoretical Background

I will try to keep this brief! Surely, you have held a whistle or a recorder before. Both work in the same way. They have a mouthpiece (M) into which you blow air. It directs the air towards the cutting edge of the labium (L), where sound is produced by the cutting of the air and the resulting vibrations.

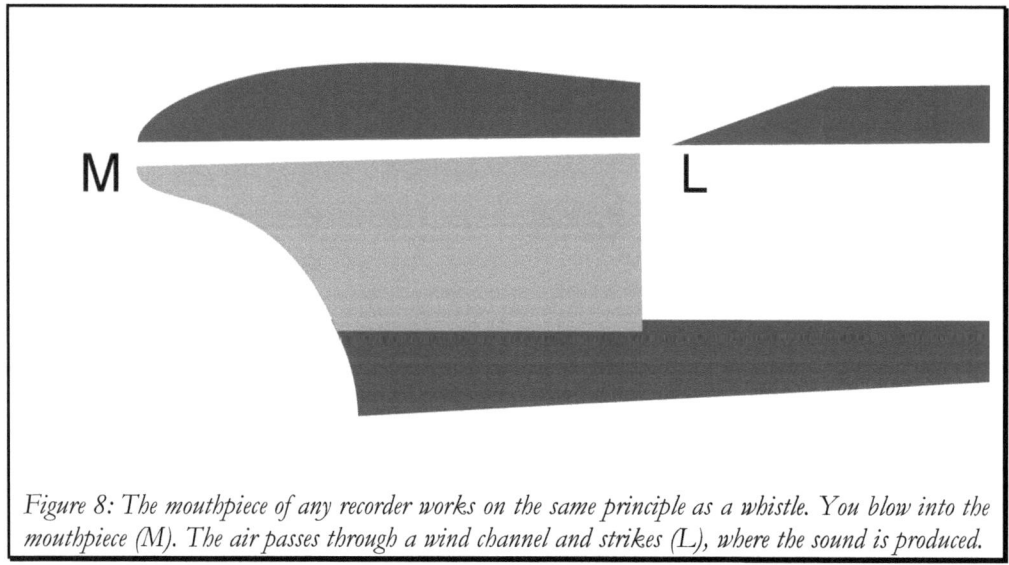

Figure 8: The mouthpiece of any recorder works on the same principle as a whistle. You blow into the mouthpiece (M). The air passes through a wind channel and strikes (L), where the sound is produced.

Thus, producing sound on a flute is child's play. As soon as a child can say "tütü" or blow "hühü," they can produce a sound on a whistle or a recorder.

Unfortunately, such a sound has little room for personal expression. Whether you blow straight or slightly angled, the air is always directed onto the labium through the wind channel. Sure, you can play softly, loudly, with a "tuuuuh" or "puuuh," but that is about it. This is not the case with the Kawala. There is no mouthpiece to blow into, shaping the air through a channel onto the labium. Instead, we must shape the air ourselves.

Figure 9: Compare this image with the one on the previous page. Here, too, is point (L), where the air needs to be directed. With the Kawala, we need to find a way for the air to strike (L) to produce the sound.

Figure 10: With our mouth and lips (M), we can cover a large part of the opening and then direct the air precisely onto (L).

Practical Application

Now that you understand the concept from the sketches above, I want to show and explain a few pictures. Please read what is written under each picture in this section before implementing it. It will help you produce a clean tone as quickly as possible.

The golden rule:

Figure 11: First, position the flute correctly.

Figure 12: Then, shape your mouth!

I see it time and time again. Kawala students shape their mouths before positioning the flute. Do not do this; certainly not at this stage!

The flute rests so the lower lip supports it (figure 11). Only then should you shape your lips as if you were about to say "Uuuh" (figure 12). Be patient. You will soon have the opportunity to experiment. I want to emphasize here that you should position the flute first before attempting to produce a tone.

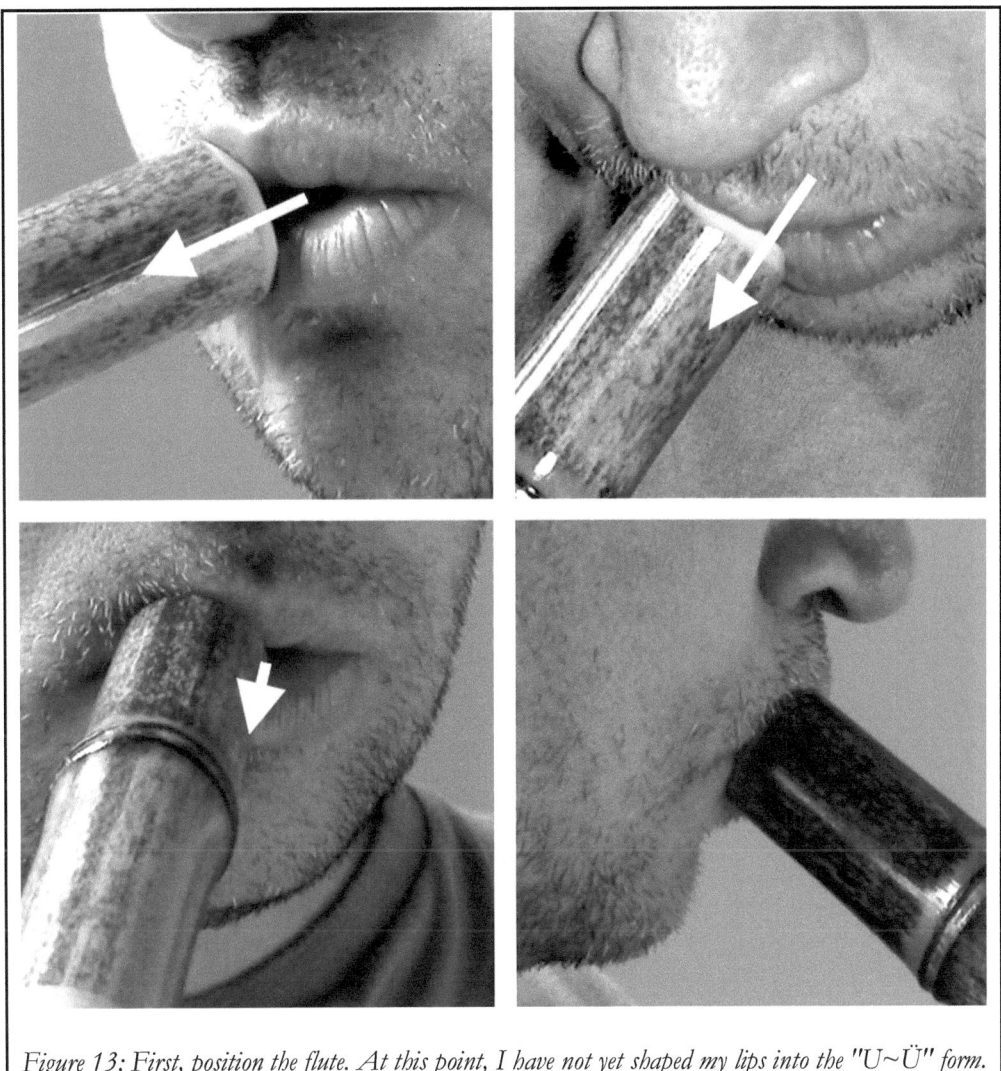

Figure 13: First, position the flute. At this point, I have not yet shaped my lips into the "U~Ü" form.

Do you see what is happening here? I position the Kawala so that it points slightly to the right. This way, it is slightly lifted on the left edge and completely sealed on the right side.

The Correct Blowing Angle

Figure 14: The ideal blowing angle

In this photo, my index finger points to a straight line, indicating where my nose points when I hold the flute. It is best to sit in front of a mirror and try to apply everything you have read so far. Remember: a 30-40 cm (11.8-15.8 in) tube is sufficient; you do not need a flute to practice producing sound. However, you must be able to generate a tone to turn a tube into a flute!

The Correct Position

Figure 15 to the right illustrates the concept. (M) represents your mouth. Press the flute to your lips and shape them as if you are about to say "Ooooh."

And now blow a stream of air (L).

The edge of the flute should cut this air stream.

The stream should not be too wide or too narrow. It requires experimentation and practice.

Below is an excellent exercise to create a steady and correctly sized air stream that you can try right now:

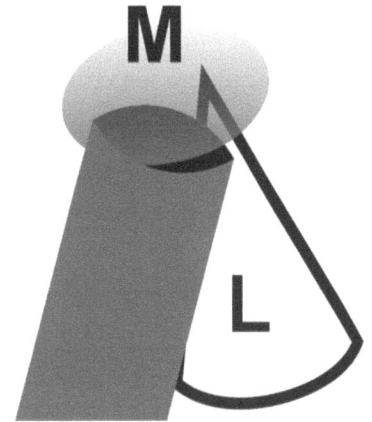

Figure 15: The correct position.

Figure 16: Exercise I.: Forming your mouth and position.

In the left photo, I am whistling. Although I try to whistle straight ahead, you can see in the picture that I tend to whistle to the right. In the second photo, you can see how I push my lips to the right. Usually, this prevents you from whistling properly. It is like trying to blow out a birthday candle on your right shoulder without moving your head. Try this in the opposite direction, then return to the center.

Next, take your right hand and form a ring with your index finger and thumb. First, position the ring so that the air passes through it. Then, move your hand slightly to the right so you feel the air stream hitting the tips of your index finger and thumb. This is where the sound is generated in the tube.

You should not blow only into the flute but also not just over it. Half of the air stream should go into the flute, and the other half should flow out.

The ratio is about 50-50; as the ratio shifts to more air outside the flute, the pitch becomes higher. The tone will be lower if more air goes into the flute.

Figure 17: The blowing angle on the left would produce a C#, the one in the middle a C, and the one on the right a B.

These three images demonstrate that you can play the same tube a half step higher or lower. You can rotate the flute to the right by maintaining the same head position to raise the pitch. Bringing the flute closer to the body's central axis will lower the pitch.

Of course, you can achieve the same effect by constantly holding the flute in one direction and instead swiveling your head back and forth. The true art lies in not swiveling the head or flute too much but balancing everything a bit — even influencing pitch with the lips.

Use your lips to adjust the tone with your lips or mouth shape, and blow more air without moving the flute or your head. Imagine giving a kiss with a stiff neck to see how flexible your lips can be. This technique lets you increase air pressure for a lower pitch or direct more air outside the flute for a higher pitch.

Figure 18: The lips form an "oo" shape, producing sound at the notch.	*Figure 19: Without moving your head or the flute, the lips and mouth are angled more towards the flute because I am blowing more air into it.*

Of course, I am exaggerating in Figures 18 and 19 to illustrate the concept. In reality, you will only need to make subtle adjustments. You can control the airflow by adjusting the flute, tilting your head, and shaping your lips.

Everyone tends to develop his or her style. For instance, I prefer holding the flute towards pointing to the floor and tilting my head slightly over it, rather than as shown in the images. While I use lip shape and flute movement to vary and bend the sound, this positioning allows me to make nuanced adjustments by tilting my head.

Figure 20: The pitch is also raised by adjusting the lips to blow more air over the edge.

The essentials have been covered. Now, you just need to get a flute and start practicing. Kep in mind that you can adjust the pitch of each note using at least one of the three techniques: tilting your head, moving the flute, or shaping your lips.

When building your flute, ensure the holes are drilled and tuned so that the middle position produces the correct pitch. If you hold the flute at a too steep angle, it might be tuned correctly for that position, but it will sound out of tune if you play it more centrally. So, practice for a few hours to produce an excellent sound and tune your flute correctly.

It is not difficult, but it requires some practice and perseverance.

Basic Knowledge: The Major Scale

On the keyboard (see figure 1 above), you have 12 keys from "C" to "B." The classic major scale is the C major scale: C-D-E-F-G-A-B-C.

However, additional notes exist in between, such as C# or F#. When listing all the notes sequentially, you have 12 notes in total. The interval between two consecutive notes is always a half step. For example, the interval from C to C# is a half step, and from C# to D is a half step. Therefore, the transition from C to D spans a whole step.

The major scale follows the pattern Whole-Whole-Half-Whole-Whole-Whole-Half. For the C major scale, this is understood as:

C	C#	D	D#	E	F	F#	G	G#	A	A#	B
Whole											
		Whole									
				Half							
					Whole						
							Whole				
									Whole		

The last half step, from B to C, is not shown here. I find calculating such a scale quite cumbersome, especially when our goal is simply to identify the notes we need to drill to build a well-tuned flute.

Therefore, I created a table that some of you might recognize from my previous books (German readers). I use this table to calculate my scales. It is important to note that the root note is always assigned the number "0".

Take a look at the table below. I have listed all the notes on the keyboard across two octaves and marked the notes of the C major scale in **bold** with a cross (**X**) underneath for clarity.

C	C#	D	D#	E	F	F#	G	G#	A	A#	B
X		X		X	X		X		X		X
C	**C#**	**D**	**D#**	**E**	**F**	**F#**	**G**	**G#**	**A**	**A#**	**B**
X											

We can now create a formula from this. To do so, we place a "0" under the root note and assign each subsequent note in the scale a number representing the number of steps we need to jump.

C	C#	D	D#	E	F	F#	G	G#	A	A#	B
0		2		2	1		2		2		2
C	**C#**	**D**	**D#**	**E**	**F**	**F#**	**G**	**G#**	**A**	**A#**	**B**
1											

Thus, we have derived the major scale formula for our table: **0-2-2-1-2-2-2-1**. And what does this **0-2-2-1-2-2-2-1** formula mean for flute making?
It simplifies the process! For example, if you have cut a tube to play the root note E, you can quickly calculate the E major scale before drilling the holes. Just use the table, enter "0" for E, and continue with the formula:

C	C#	D	D#	E	F	F#	G	G#	A	A#	B
				0		2		2	1		2
C	C#	D	D#	E	F	F#	G	G#	A	A#	B
	2		2	1							

There are countless different scales. The major scale is one of the heptatonic scales (scales with seven notes). Along with the minor scales, which are also heptatonic, it is the most commonly used in our circles. For building a Kawala, the major scale is crucial because it forms the basis for calculating the hole positions, even if you want to tune your flute to a different scale. At the end of this book, I will show you how to build any imaginable scale on a Kawala based on the major scale. You should know the 0-2-2-1-2-2-2-1 formula as well as your phone number!

Fingering Chart for the Kawala in Major Scale

Playing the Kawala flute is very simple. The lowest note, the "root note," is produced by closing all the holes. You simply open one hole at a time to ascend the major scale. For the highest note, B, you will notice that I have closed hole number 5 (counted from the bottom). It is because you could not hold the flute properly, as you need at least one thumb and one additional finger to grip it.

Of course, you can also play intermediate notes. For instance, to play D#, start by fingering E and then close the lowest hole. It will lower the pitch slightly. If this does not produce the desired D#, you can blow a bit more air into the flute than usual.

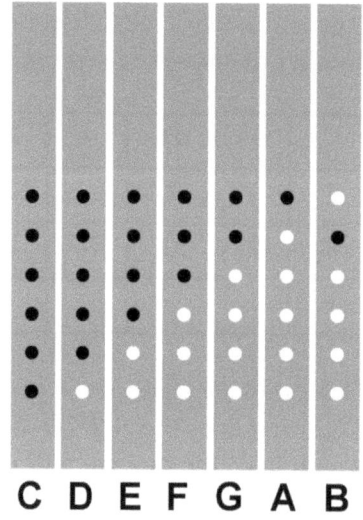

C D E F G A B

Figure 21: Fingering Chart.

The following are some explanatory images of the major scale of the Kawala. We will use a Kawala tuned to E major for this demonstration.

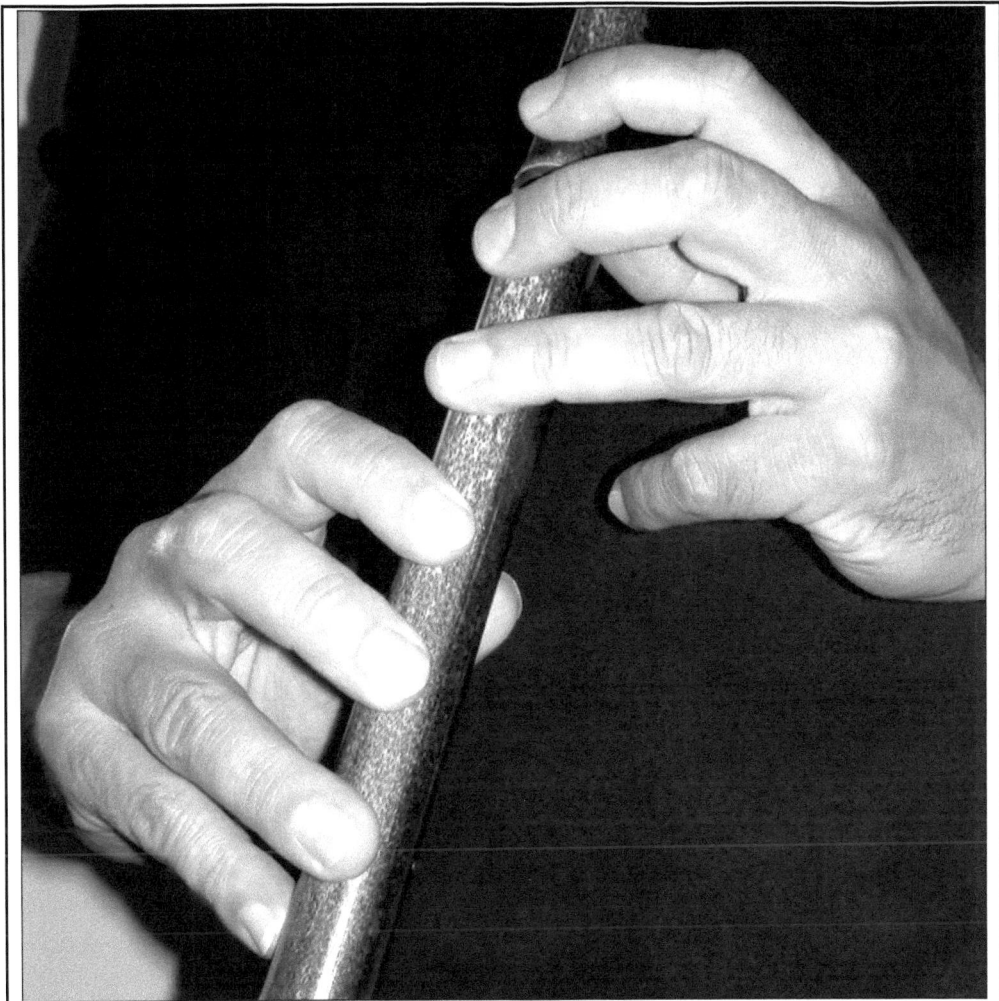

Figure 22: (The Note E). Make sure that when you play the flute to the right, as shown here, your right hand is positioned lower. Also, pay attention to the small finger supporting below.

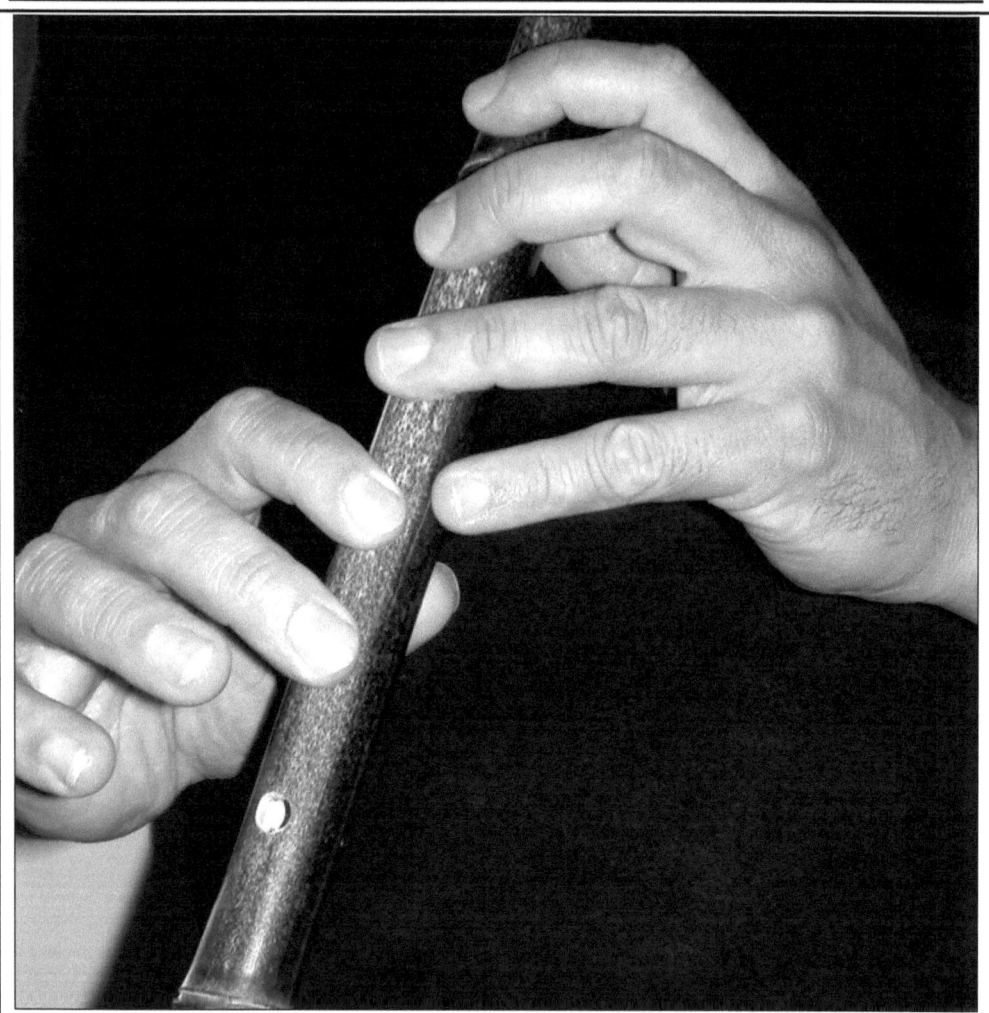

Figure 23: (The note F#). Notice how I have lifted my right hand's pinky and ring fingers below. Now, my left pinky finger supports the flute from above. I was not aware of this until I saw these photos. The key takeaway is that we must always support the Kawala so that we can press the blowing edge firmly with our lips without the Kawala slipping.

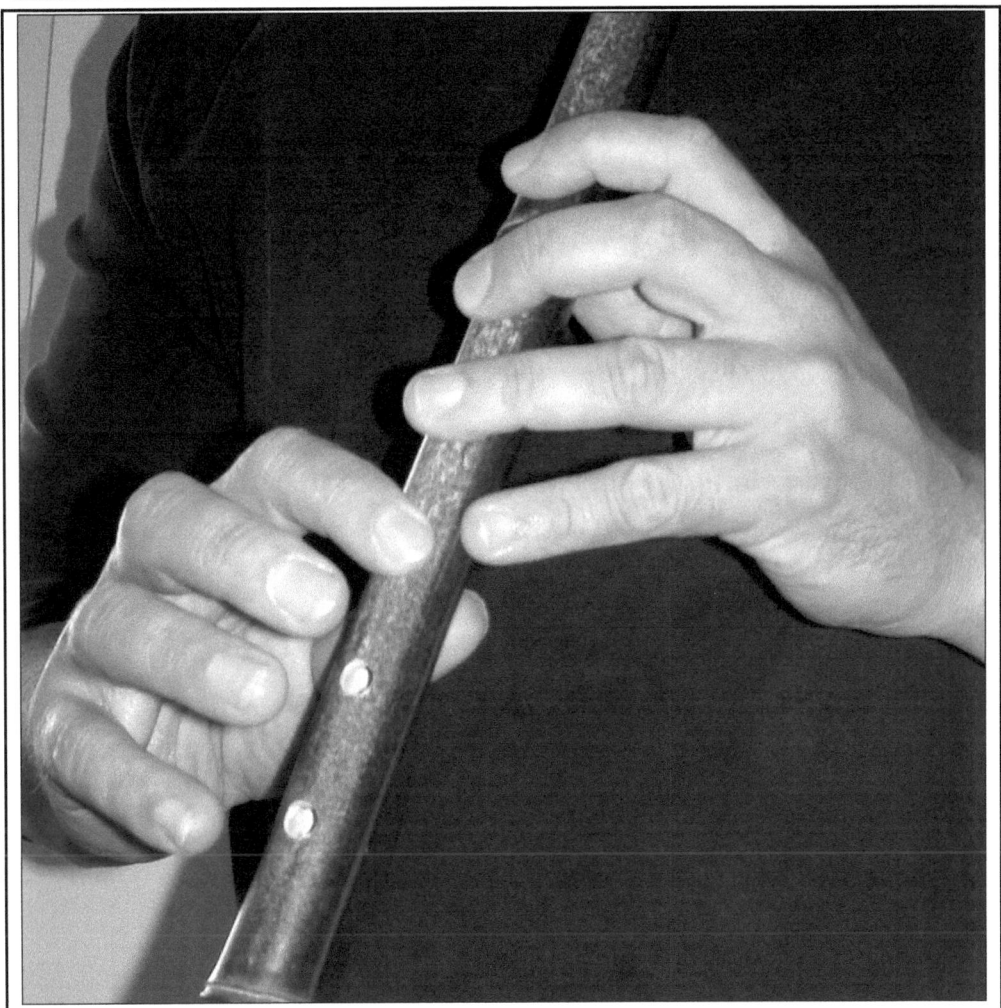

Figure 24: (The note G#). Even with G#, I have lifted my right pinky finger. I can still support the flute with my right index finger and thumb from below. The left hand is positioned the same as with F#.

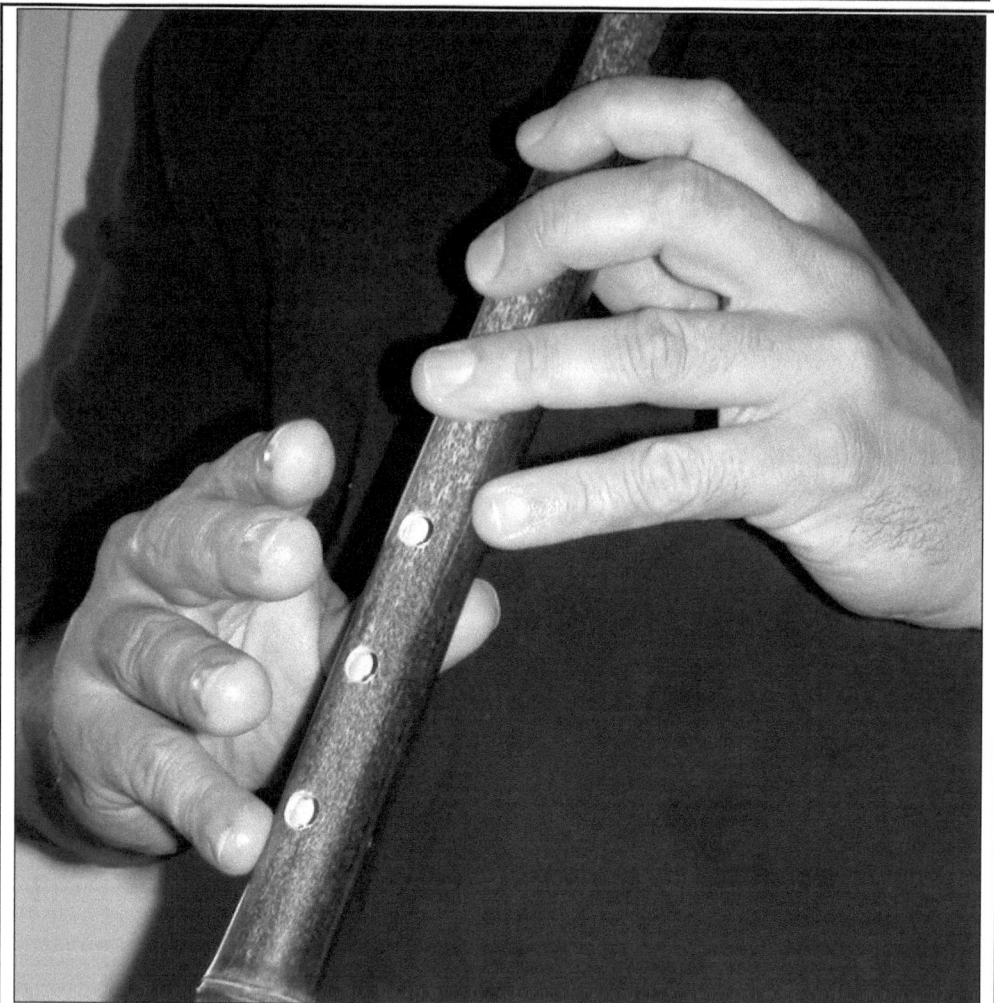

Figure 25: (The note A). The right hand does not have a role in sound production. All the holes that the right hand would close are open! However, without this hand, the Kawala would very likely be pushed to the right by the pressure from the lips, as this hand's thumb and pinky finger support the flute while playing.

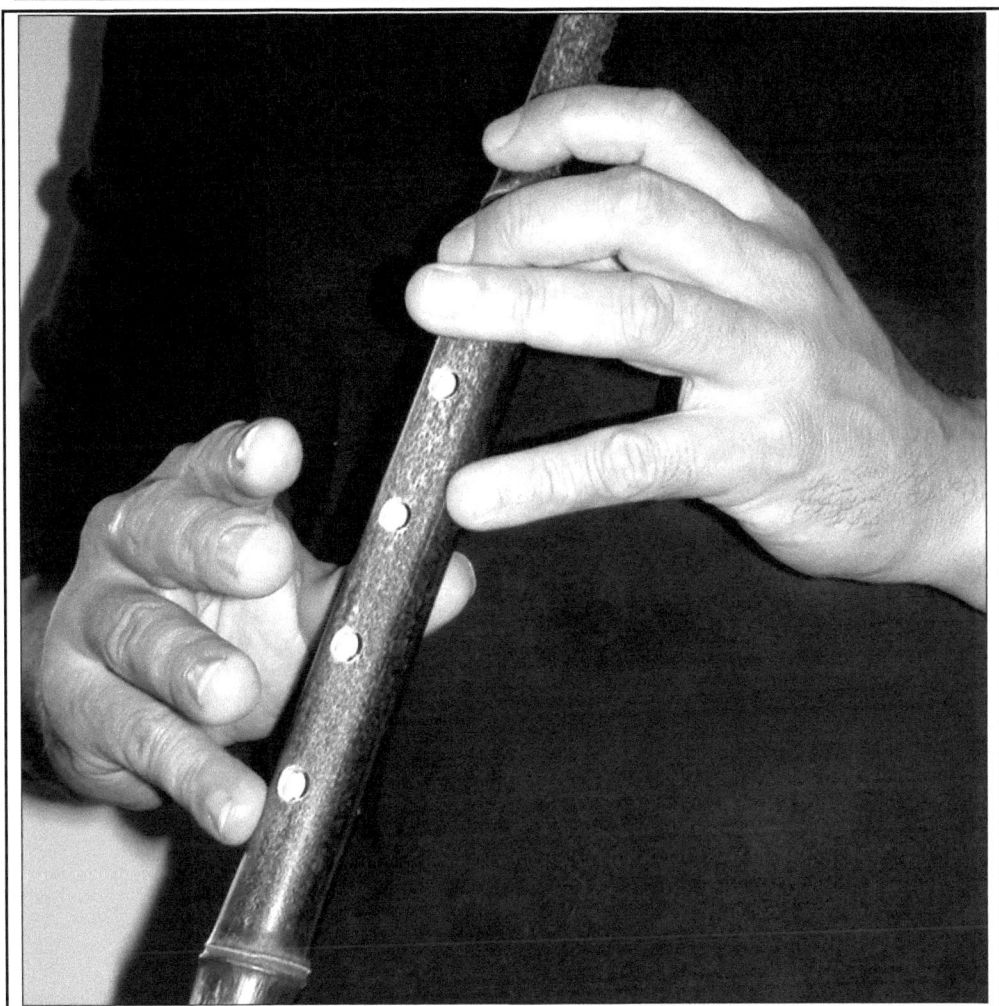

Figure 26: (The note B). The golden rule applies here as well: hold the flute firmly! We only have a few support points left. Therefore, the right hand's pinky finger has now become very important.

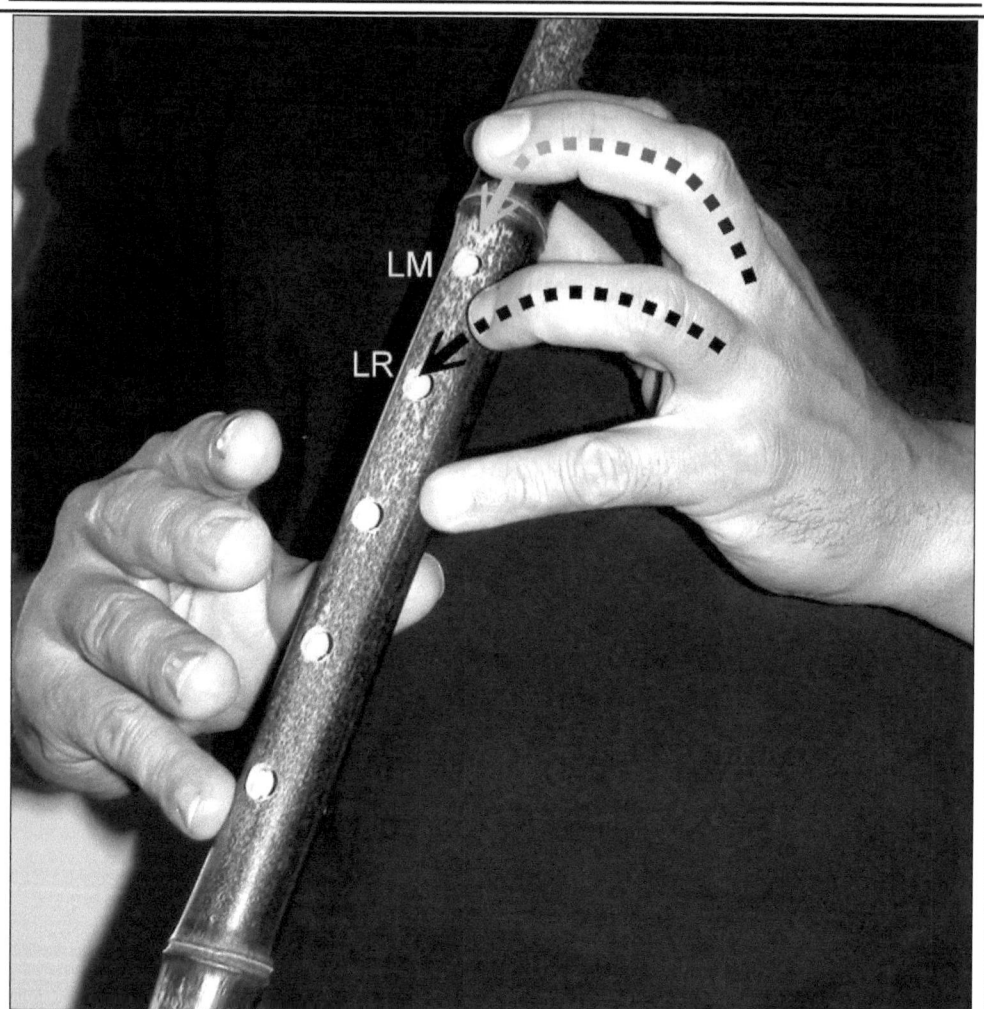

Figure 27: (The note C#). The sixth note on the Kawala, here C#, really needs practice. Please look at the picture. The left ring finger (LR) is lifted but not positioned directly over the corresponding hole. This is necessary; otherwise, the left ring finger would not have enough support. The left middle finger (LM) is lifted relatively high here to show the hole below in the picture. Usually, I do not lift the middle finger this high. Therefore, the only support points left are the two fingers of the right hand below, the pinky finger on top, the index finger (hidden behind the middle finger in the picture), and the left thumb.

Figure 28: (The note D#). Theoretically, all holes should be open for the seventh note of the major scale on a Kawala. This is extremely difficult. Therefore, I place the middle finger back on the corresponding hole. It makes the F# about 5 cents lower, but it is not noticeable, and if necessary, the tone can be corrected using the techniques mentioned above.

Playing the Second Octave

You can play more than seven notes and the sounds in between on a Kawala. However, you need to reach the second octave for this. The individual notes of the second octave are fingered the same way as in the first octave. You initially need to blow a little harder to reach the second octave.

The problem with this approach is that the sound changes suddenly. Not only does each note become slightly sharp, but the music also gets louder. The better method is to narrow the airstream while keeping the same air pressure.

Think of the images (Figure 16), where you should form a ring with your thumb and middle finger. Now, imagine making this ring smaller. You might be familiar with this from blowing out candles. If it does not work immediately, you narrow the airstream so that the air hits the flame more precisely. Think of this while trying to hit the second octave on your Kawala! The more you practice, the more natural and easier it becomes. Here is an exercise I recommend for training air control:

Step 1

    a. Inhale deeply, but not to the point of straining your lungs, as that costs too much energy. Simply take a quick and deep breath.
    b. Whisper while exhaling: "puh, puh, puh, puh..." (a French "u")
    c. Pay attention to how the air flows through your lips.
    d. You should be able to whisper "puh" between 25 and 35 times.

Step 2

    a. Repeat Step 1 (a-d), but make the "u" a little longer (count in your mind until 3)
    b. Now, while the air flows between your lips, try pressing them together slightly and then relaxing them. It feels like you have a lentil between your lips.
    c. Once you feel you can control the airstream, try shaping your lips as if you were going to say "oo" during the long"puh" part.

Step 3

    a. Repeat Step 2, and this time, focus on ensuring the pressure comes from your diaphragm.

    b. The air flowing from your lungs remains constant, but the airstream becomes stronger by making the gap between your lips smaller (like pressing on a lentil).

    c. Now, instead of whispering "puh," whisper "<ueh."
The "<" symbol is not a typo; it represents a sound that cannot be described with letters. Imagine a soft cough. You do not say "pueh, pueh, pueh" or "kueh, kueh, kueh," but rather it is the aspiration at the start of the cough – the blocking and sudden release of air: "<ueh, <ueh, <ueh."

It would help if you bought an aluminum tube with a diameter of about 20 mm from the hardware store. Cut it to 20-30 cm (7.9 -11.8 in) in length. Be sure to sand the ends with metal sandpaper to prevent splinters from cutting your lips. Wash the tube to remove metal dust, and you can carry it anywhere, even in the shower, and practice at every opportunity!

While a tube up to 50 cm (19.7 in), like the Kawala, is suitable for playing two octaves, you will quickly notice that the longer the tube, the more registers you can play. When I am in hardware stores, I often grab a 2 m copper tube and test it out. You can play up to 6 or 7 consecutive notes without drilling a single hole by controlling the air pressure with your lips.

Playing the Notes Between Notes

Let us take the E major Kawala. The fingerings for the major scale are always the same, whether in C or E. Below, I will present the fingering chart with our 0-2-2-1-2-2-2-1 formula table.

E	F	F#	G	G#	A	A#	B	C	C#	D	D#	E
0		2		2	1		2		2		2	1

As you can see from the chart, we can easily play "Twinkle Twinkle Little Star" in E major. However, for cases where, for example, a G or an A# is needed, we have to come up with something. We have a couple of options for doing this.

Playing Intermediate Notes Using the Example of Note C

As the chart on the previous page shows, we have a B and a C# on an E major Kawala. Our goal is now to play the C, which lies between these two notes. We have already discussed the following options:

1. Bend the C# to a C by blowing more air into the flute.
2. Bend the B up to a C by blowing more air over the edge of the flute.

We also remember that the same can be achieved by tilting the flute or the head and shaping the lips. This method is suitable for adding some ornamentation to the music, but if you are playing a piece with an E major Kawala that consistently requires a C, it will be very tedious to sway the flute back and forth constantly.

In principle, in almost all cases, you can flatten a note by closing lower holes. However, the key aspect for C# is that the top hole is closed, and for B, the top two holes are closed. If you leave the second hole (from the top) open and close a few holes below, the note will be slightly lower, usually by a half step, which generally gives you a C.

The other, more challenging (but most reliable) method is to half-close the hole below the C#, which is the second hole. Doing this is not always easy, as you might accidentally close it three-quarters of the way, producing the quarter tones typical of Arabic music but not the C.

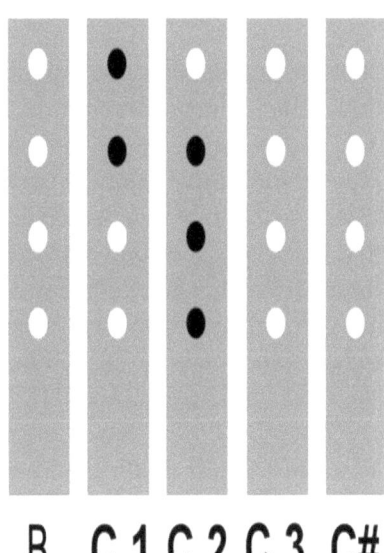

Figure 29: Different Fingerings for a C

However, there is a method that makes half-closing relatively simple and gives the sound an oriental flavor. Compare the following two images.

On the right, you can see how to half-close (shade) with the index finger.

In the case of our E major Kawala, this would give us a slightly lower A, but not yet a G#. It would be the Arabic quarter-tone A♭, which does not exist in Western music.

Still, you can use it as a sound ornament, allowing the finger to gradually slide down until it completely covers the hole to produce a G#.

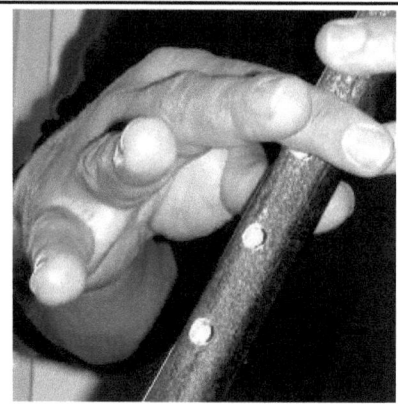

Figure 30: Half-holding.

Half-closing needs to be practiced. It is best to practice it by playing up and down the scale with each hole.

Here is the simple method I mentioned above. Place two fingers together over the hole so that the air escapes between them. The air is then sufficiently obstructed at the exit, allowing you to play a half-step lower note. Slowly slide down, and your index finger will eventually cover the hole completely.

You can use this method with almost any hole. You would need to use your middle and ring fingers for the second hole from the bottom. It becomes problematic only with the bottom hole. While you can use your middle and ring

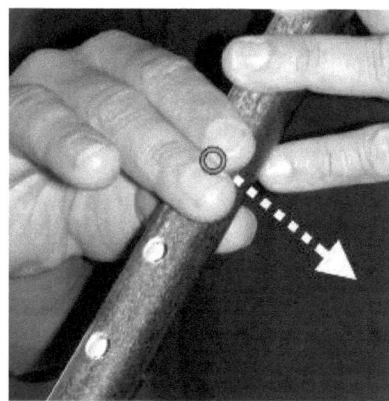

Figure 31: Two-Finger method.

fingers for the second-to-last hole, it is challenging for the lowest hole because the middle finger is already occupied.

Build your First Professional Kawala

Finally, the time has come! You now possess the knowledge to build an advanced professional Kawala flute. I will guide you step-by-step on constructing a Kawala in G major from bamboo. You will need a few tools for this, which I will list in the instructions. I recommend reading through everything here and reflecting on it before building the Kawala.

Step 1: Preparing the Bamboo Tube

Admittedly, finding a suitable bamboo tube is somewhat difficult. Bamboo tubes from hardware stores are usually thick-walled with a small inner diameter, designed to be used in the garden without rotting. I have had good experiences with garden torches made from bamboo, which have thin walls and an excellent inner diameter for flutes. However, I am always on the lookout and have national and international suppliers for my tubes, and I suggest you will have to do the same. It took me some time until my suppliers understood what I needed and did not.

For the Kawala tube, you should generally pay attention to four things:

1. The inner diameter should be between 18-22 mm.
2. The wall thickness should be 3-4 mm.
3. The tube should not have any cracks.
4. If possible, it should be from the lower part of the bamboo reed because the higher parts have grooves where the leaves grow.

In the picture, I am working with a tube of bamboo Nigra with a wall thickness of 3 mm and an inner diameter of 18.5 mm. Bamboo has a fibrous shell that can splinter when sawing. Therefore, I tape a painter's masking tape around the spot where I will cut the bamboo to the desired length.

You should also cut bamboo with a pull saw (Japanese saw). I have tried everything imaginable, and a Japanese saw is incomparable!

Here, I am sawing the tube to a suitable length. Generally, I leave the tube a bit longer than the expected final size. The expected final size for a Kawala in G is about 39 cm (15.4 in). It depends on the tube's diameter and the bamboo wall's thickness. Therefore, I initially cut this tube to about 41-42 cm (16.15-16.5 in).

To achieve a straight cut, I rotate the tube while sawing. In the picture on the right, it almost looks like I am sawing off my thumb, but this is not the case. However, even after years, I occasionally get injuries when I am not focusing, so go out and buy suitable work gloves! If you intend to do this professionally for a living, you will have to invest in a high-quality band saw sooner or later.

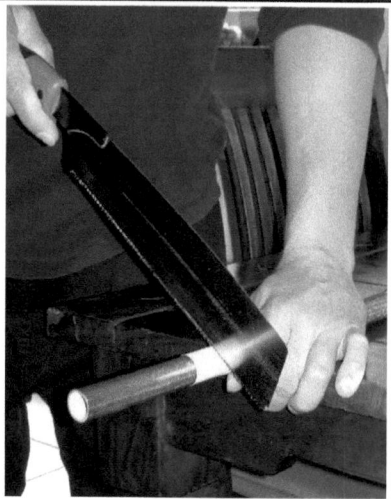

Figure 32: Japanese saw for bamboo.

Important Note:

Wear gloves, especially when building a flute with your children. I am not wearing gloves in the pictures, so you can see what I am doing more clearly.

Now, you should work on the inside of the tube. Bamboo has chambers separated by membranes. In the picture on the right, I have split a bamboo tube lengthwise, and you can see a membrane in the middle of the tube that would obstruct the airflow.

We need to remove this membrane!

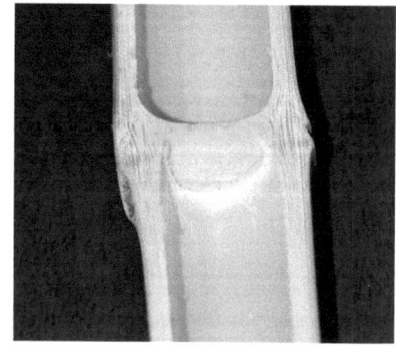

Figure 33: A bamboo membrane.

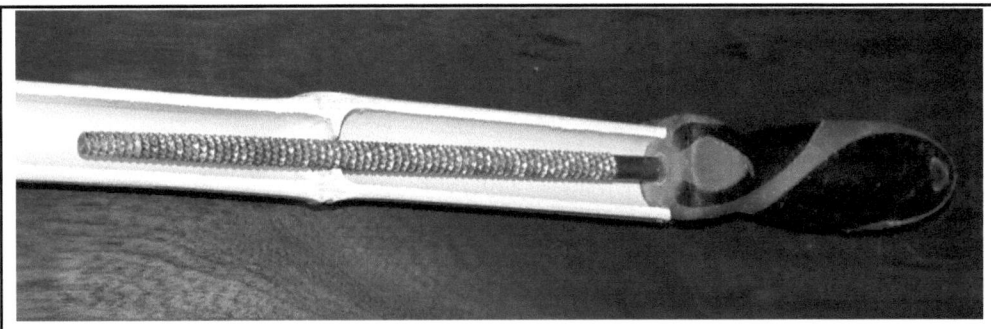

Figure 34: It is pretty easy to pierce through the membranes with a coarse round file. I hold the tube in my left hand and move it back and forth until I no longer feel any resistance.

Depending on how many chambers your bamboo tube has, you must file away two to three membranes for a Kawala in G (about 39 cm (15.4 in)).

It is best to have two round files: a coarse one and a fine one for smoothing the inside of the bamboo tube. If you want it to be smooth, attach sandpaper at the end to a 0.5 cm (0.2 in) diameter rod and smooth the bamboo inside. If you want it perfect, you can attach this rod to a power drill and achieve an even smoother interior wall. However, be aware that the first few tubes might get damaged until you know how to properly hold or secure the tube.

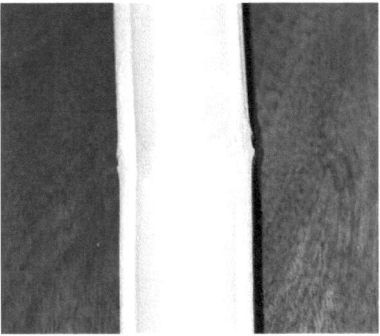

Figure 35: A filed-down membrane.

Step 2: Sanding the Blowing Edge

The Kawala must have a sharp blowing edge all around. It should not be so sharp that it injures your lips while playing, but it should be sharp enough to direct your breath precisely onto the edge. If the edge is too blunt, producing a good sound will not be easy.

However, as a flute maker, you can alter the sound's timbre and quality by adjusting the edge's characteristics.

The sharper the edge, the brighter the sound. I prefer an edge thickness of about 1-1.5 mm (about 0.04 -0.06 inches).

Figure 36: The blowing edge

For instance, the Turkish version of the Ney has a horn or plastic attachment, making it easier to have a very sharp edge. However, this comes with the drawback of moisture accumulating in the attachment socket. Furthermore, the goal is to build the oldest form of Kawala and Ney, which did not use such add-ons.

It is also crucial not to sand the edge to the point where it almost resembles a pencil. For example, "A" is the better option in the image on the right. "B," on the other hand, would result in the edge becoming too fragile and prone to breaking.

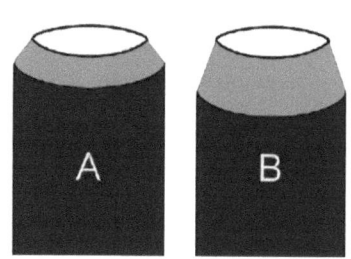

Figure 37: Good Edge - Bad Edge

Sanding the edge itself is relatively straightforward. I use a grinding plate for my cordless drill. Such an attachment does not cost much and can always be helpful around the house. Some cordless drills even come along with a grinding plate. However, it would help to have a cordless drill with a high rotation speed and preferably a spare battery. Nothing is more frustrating than stopping work because the battery is not charged anymore. I have tried many cordless drills and realized that while a high-quality cordless drill may be more expensive, it usually lasts longer, has better batteries, and offers a more extended warranty in most cases.

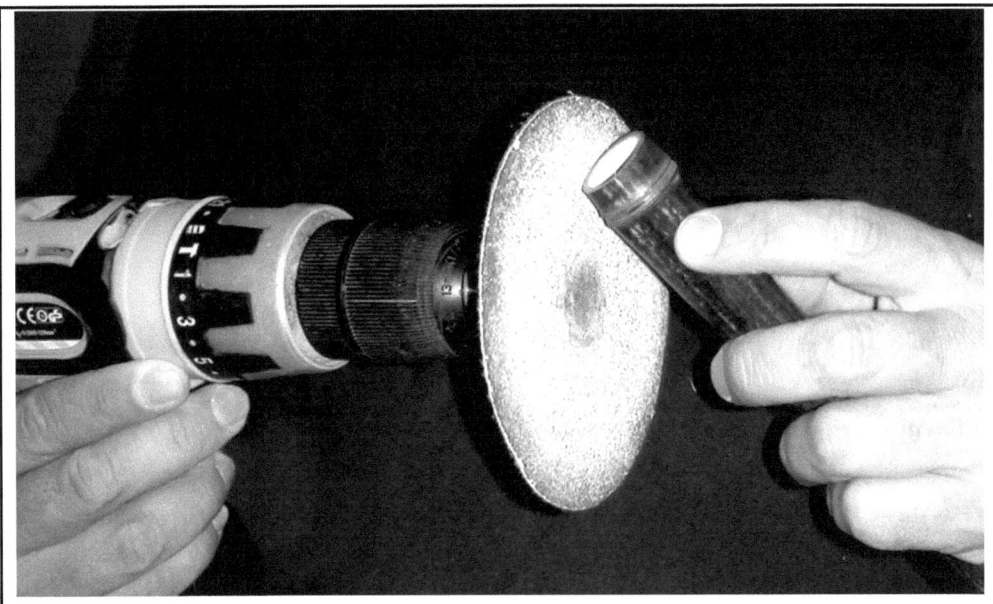

Figure 38: Sanding the blowing edge into the right shape.

It is a good idea to start with coarse sandpaper and then use fine-grain sandpaper to finish the edge. Often, the inside of the blowing edge is uneven or not smooth. You should use a piece of fine-grain sandpaper to even it out. It is absolutely unpleasant to get a splinter in your lips!

Important Note:

Make the blowing edge at the end of the tube where the inner diameter is the largest. The difference should not be too big. If the blowing edge has an inner diameter of 18 mm (7.08 in), the other end of the flute can often be between 16.5 and 18 mm (6.5 and 7.08 in). In any case, if there is one, you should make the blowing edge at the wider end. If both ends are the same size, it will also function.

Tuning the Fundamental Note of the Kawala

Listen up! Almost every mistake in building a Kawala can be corrected, except if you ruin the fundamental note. That is why this section is significant. We have assumed you have already cut the tube to approximately 42 cm (16.5 in). You have also finished the blowing edge and learned how to produce a clean tone. So, take the tube in your hand and see which note is played.

You will need a couple of burning rods (how to make these is explained below) and a chromatic tuner, which you can get for about 15 euros online. You can also download a free tuner app on your smartphone. Additionally, there are many online and downloadable tuners for your PC. However, I do not recommend drilling or sanding bamboo near your PC. It will make a massive mess of dust, and your computer will not appreciate it in the long run.

As mentioned, we want to build a Kawala in G here. It is about 39-41 cm (15.4 – 16.1 in) in length. So, when you play your prepared tube, you will probably see either a sharp-tuned F or an F# on your tuner. The shorter the reed, the higher the tun; thus, keep shortening your flute until you have a clean G

You can skip the following section if you know how to work with a tuner. Otherwise, you should read this section.

What Tuners Are Good For

A tuner is a device or application that detects and shows the pitch of musical notes produced on an instrument using electronics. It enables musicians to confirm that their instrument is properly tuned by indicating whether a note is too high (sharp) or too low (flat) compared to the desired pitch. What you need is a chromatic tuner. It detects all 12 chromatic scale notes, making it versatile enough to tune any instrument.

You would tighten or loosen the strings for string instruments. Regarding bamboo flutes, the notes must be tuned during the manufacturing process. They cannot be re-tuned, or only under significant circumstances. Therefore, great care is required from the flute maker.

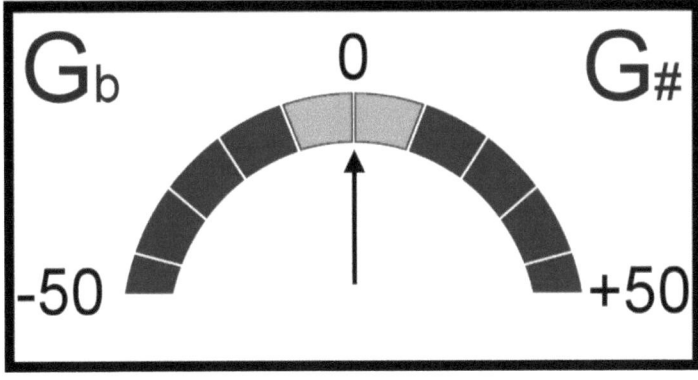

Figure 39: Perfectly tuned to G between the Gb and G#.

This illustration shows the basic principle of all tuners. When, for instance, aiming to play a G, then G# is to the right, and Gb is to the left. Most tuners light up when a G is played correctly. However, I placed a zero in the center to highlight negative and positive cent values. If the note is too low, the needle (or arrow) points to Gb; if it is too high, it points to G#. If the flute is entirely out of tune, the tuner shows a different note, such as an E, about one and a half steps below the desired G.

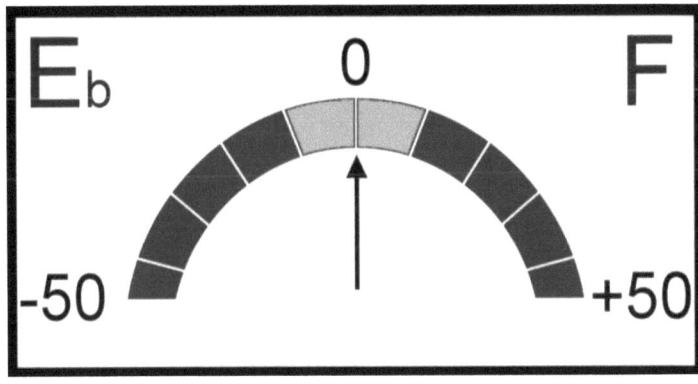

Figure 40: The perfect E (between Eb and F), but we want a G!

49

Figure 40 shows us that we are far below our target. If we want a G and our tuner says, "Hey buddy, you are playing an E," you should quickly count how far G is from E. Think: E – F – Gb – G

That is three steps away. So, you must start shortening your instrument to reach your goal of a higher note.

Hz and Cents

There is something else you should know to understand the explanations in this book. All notes have a specific relationship to each other. If we define a particular sound as C, the other notes relate to this sound in a particular ratio. If ten people were to hide in different rooms and each sing and record "Twinkle Twinkle Little Star," probably no two recordings would be identical. This leads to the necessity of agreeing on where C begins. Most flutes are tuned to 440 Hz or 432 Hz, which you can also set on your tuner.

The notes are further divided into cents.

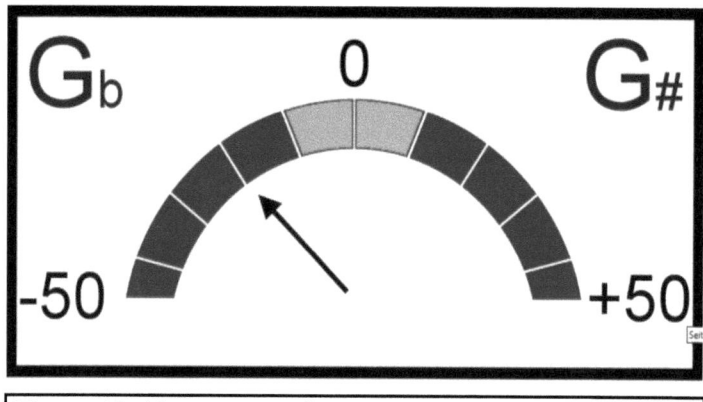

Figure 41: 20 cents too flat (or too low).

For example, you can see above that the arrow does not point to "0" for the G but is slightly to the left, indicating it is 20 cents flat. The light gray area around zero is where the sound is considered acceptable. Usually, people cannot discern whether a "G" is two or three cents higher or lower, but they can notice a difference if it is 15 or more than 25 cents mistuned when all other notes are in tune.

Now that we have clarified how the tuner works, you should remember a few basic note rules:

Basic Note Rule I:

The fundamental note of a tube changes by about a half step for every 2.5-3 cm (0.98-1.18 in) change in length

---

If a 39 cm (15.35 in) tube gives you a G, you can roughly assume that cutting it down to 36 cm (14.17 in) will likely give you a G# as the fundamental note. This is just an approximation, but it is worth keeping in mind.

Take the tube you have prepared, set your tuner, and start playing. Tilt the Kawala as right as possible, then as left as possible, before resting in the between to ensure you are playing the middle tone—not too high or too low.

Let us assume our tube is 45 cm (17.71 in) long instead of the planned 42 cm (16.53 in). We would then probably have F as the fundamental note. We will now go through the steps to tune the fundamental note to G. If you have an F and want a G note, think: "After F comes F#, and then the desired G."

If you are not yet completely familiar with musical notes, write down the following on a piece of paper:

F – F# – G.

That is two steps. The Basic Note Rule I (see the box above) suggests: "Just cut off 2x3 cm (2.36 in) to get a G."

Unfortunately, this may only be accurate about 80% of the time. What do you do if this tube behaves differently? What if you cut off 6 cm (2.36 in), and the flute ends up too short? Correcting this is not straightforward!

Therefore, you should also learn the second rule.

Basic Note Rule II:

It is better to cut the flute too long than too short!

Therefore, you will be cautious and only cut off 4.5 cm (1.77 in), and do not forget the painter's masking tape! If you are lucky, the tube will be in tune after the first cut. I can tell you that this is rarely the case!

Most likely, your tuner will show the following result:

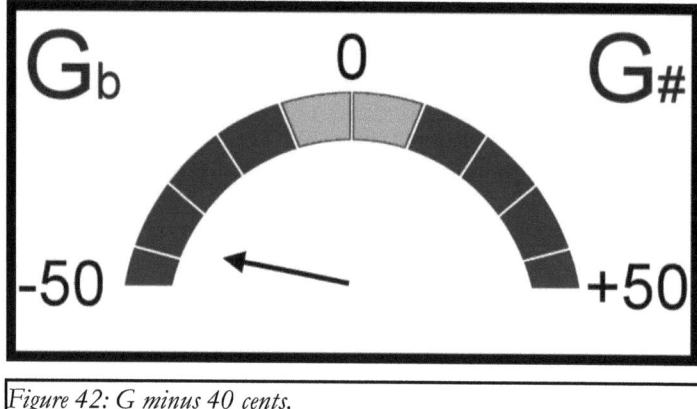

Figure 42: G minus 40 cents.

That is too flat. Be courageous and cut the tube another 1 cm (0.39 in) shorter. Now it is 39.5 cm (15.55) and gives the following result:

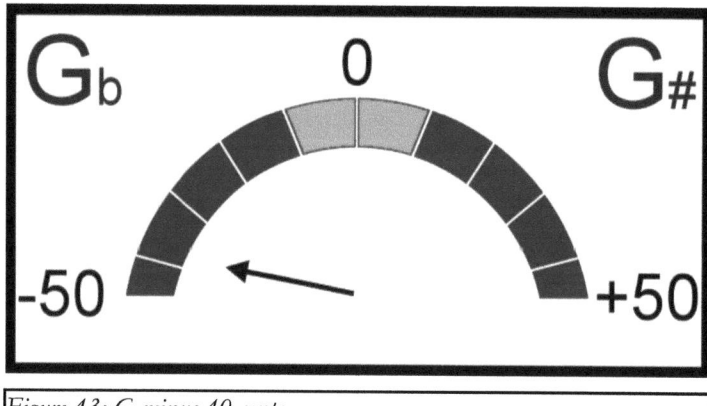

Figure 43: G minus 40 cents.

So you have reached the point where you are unsure whether you should cut any more. You certainly do not want to cut your first tube too short!

The solution is the third basic note rule.

Basic Note Rule III:

Never remove the last few cents with a saw, but rather with your grinding plate and cordless drill. Be careful not to splinter the bamboo shell.

Once you have reached the fundamental note, you can start measuring the flute to drill the finger holes. However, I first would like to talk a little about "fine-tuning" the flute.

Fine-Tuning the Flute

Generally, in all rim-blown flutes, the second register sounds slightly flatter than the first. Suppose you play a "D" in the first octave; in the second octave, it will probably be a "D minus 5 cents." This is not a big deal because it is a natural tone fluctuation.

The problem arises if you have tuned the first octave of your Kawala too flat, for example, by 11 cents. When playing the second octave, you could suddenly have 16 cents flat! If you are playing your flute alone, this hardly matters, but if you are playing with other musicians, this will become noticeably problematic, especially in the second octave. Of course, you could tilt the Kawala back and forth to correct the pitch, but there is a solution!

Allowing a Tolerance

Allow yourself a tolerance of +2 to +4 cents in the first octave. The second octave will then naturally be about -4 to -2 cents tuned. Both ranges fall within normal human perception and will not be perceived as out of tune.

It is what I always do, and I have honestly been asked by several professional musicians how I manage to make my bamboo flutes so precisely in tune. They are not; I only trick the ears!

Calculating and Drilling the Holes

Earlier, in "The Quick Guide to Building a Kawala," I briefly described how to calculate the holes. Here, we will take the time to discuss this in detail for our Kawala in G.

Painter's masking tape is your best friend when making bamboo flutes. You can get by without it, but I advise every beginner not to drill directly into their first 50 flutes. Instead, start by covering them with painter's tape.

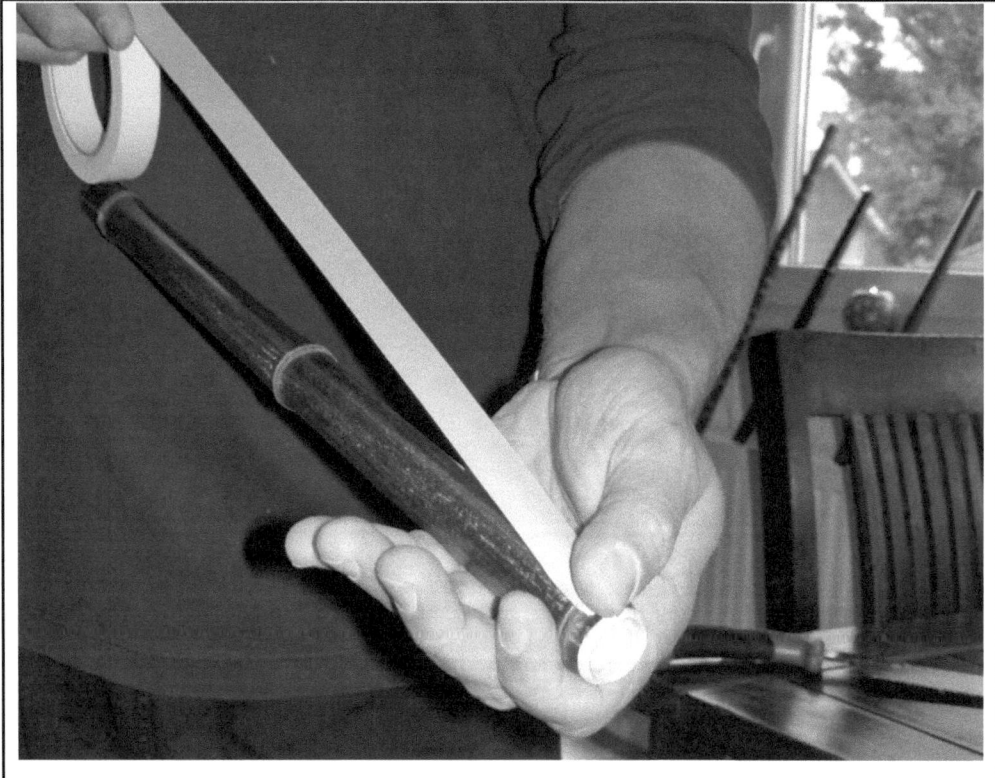

Figure 44: Apply painter's masking tape to the tube!

Buy a good-quality painter's masking tape; it must stick well and be easily re-moved. While a roll might cost several euros at the hardware store, you can often find three rolls for 1-2 euros in discount chains or supermarkets. I buy enough rolls for a whole year whenever I see such offers.

Drawing a straight line is very easy, even if you need to practice it once or twice. My right hand's middle and ring fingers press against the tube. They act as a support to prevent the pencil tip from sliding off the line on the round tube. With my left hand, I push the tube against my stomach. Then, I draw the pencil towards my "stomach," as shown in the picture above, to create a straight line. If you try to apply the central pressure on the pencil tip, you will never get a straight line.

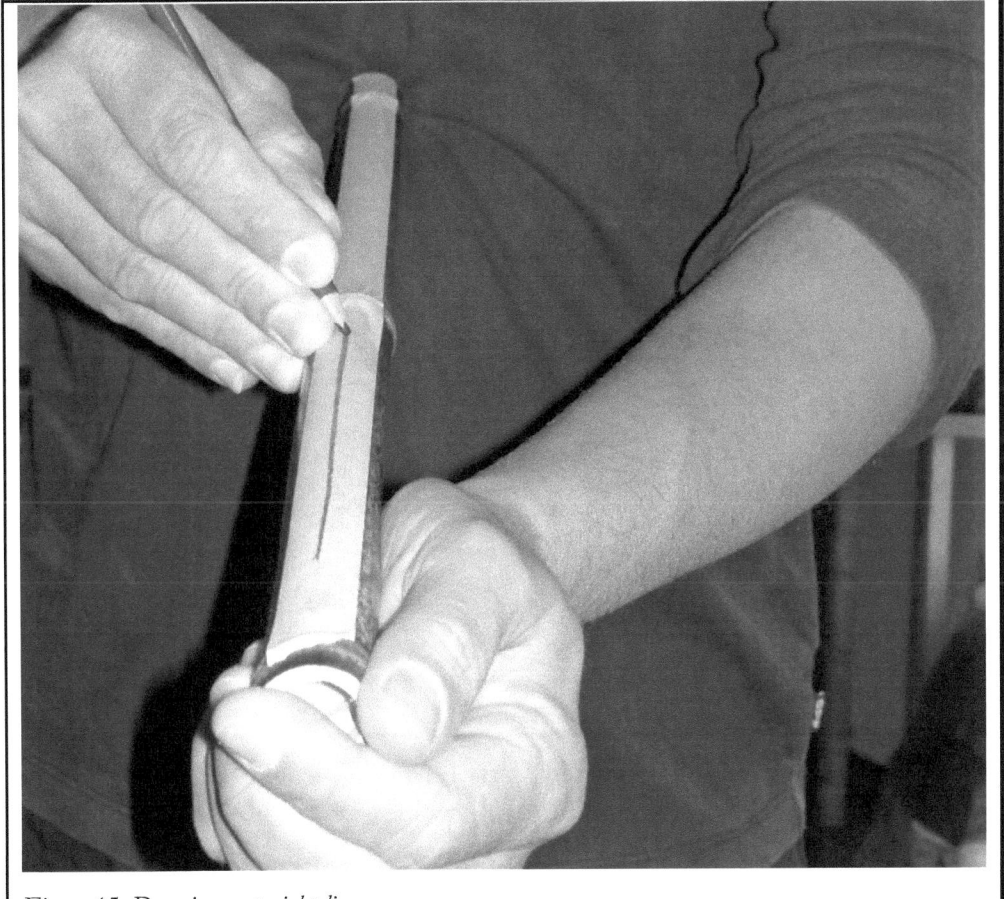

Figure 45: Drawing a straight line.

Now, you need to measure your flute again and divide the total length by 12.

For our tube, which turned out to be 39.5 cm (15.55 in) long, this means:

in cm: $39.5/12 = 3.2917$

in inches: $15.55/12 = 1.29$

Hence, 3.2917 cm (1.29 in) is the Length Variable (LV) in this case.

Write down your key number!

I cannot tell you how often I had to recalculate this number while positioning the holes because I was too lazy to write it down.

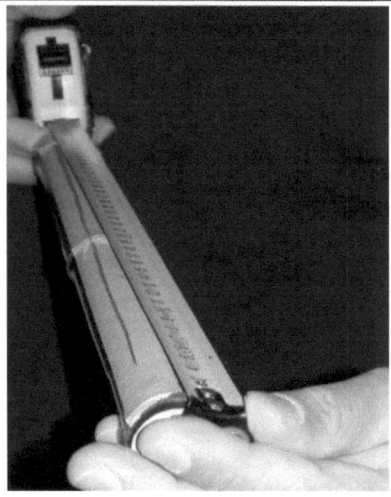

Figure 46: Measuring the tube.

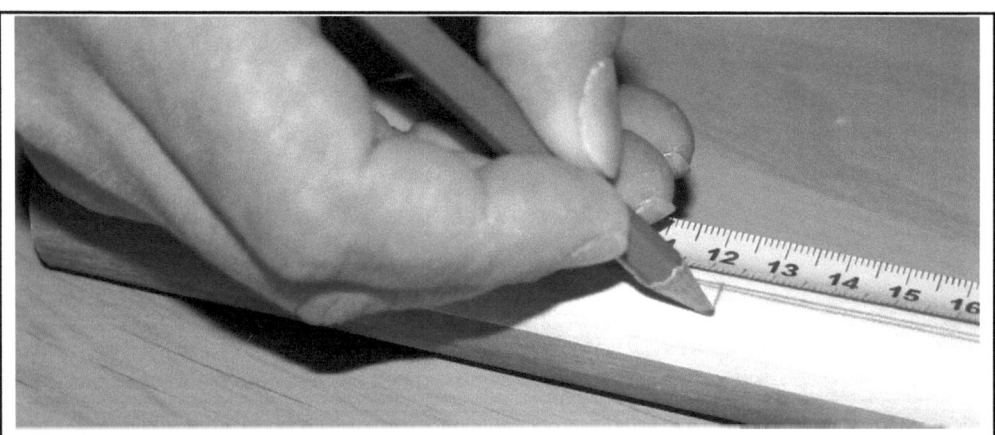

Figure 47: After calculating the positions, run a measuring tape along the line we previously drew, starting from the bottom end of the flute, and mark the positions of the holes on that line.

Now, take your pencil and mark the holes (H1 to H6) from the base of the flute toward the blowing edge (from bottom to top). For our G Kawala, the positions would be as follows: 2 LV, 3 LV, 4 LV, 5 LV, 6 LV, 7 LV.

As our LV is 3.291 cm (1.29 in), this would result in the following hole (H) positions:

- H1 = 2 x 3.291 = 6.58 cm (or H1 = 2 x 1.29 = 2.58 in)
- H2 = 3 x 3.291 = 9.87 cm (or H2 = 3 x 1.29 = 3.87 in)
- H3 = 4 x 3.291 = 13.16 cm (or H3 = 4 x 1.29 = 5.16 in)
- H4 = 5 x 3.291 = 16.46 cm (or H4 = 5 x 1.29 = 6.45 in)
- H5 = 6 x 3.291 = 19.75 cm (or H5 = 6 x 1.29 = 7.74 in)
- H6 = 7 x 3.291 = 23.04 cm (or H6 = 7 x 1.29 = 9.03 in)

H5 is important. It allows you to check whether you have miscalculated because it is always in the Kawala's middle. Even though this may seem unnecessary due to the simplicity of the calculations, it is always better to double-check.

Remember!

Hole Nr. 5 (H5) is always exactly at the midpoint of the flute's length!

Drilling the Holes

Now comes the exciting part, which is also somewhat dangerous. Even though I do not wear gloves in the following pictures, you should get a good pair. At the very least, the hand holding the bamboo tube should be protected with a thick glove while you hold the cordless drill with the other hand.

If you want to be safe, invest in a high-quality drill press. Drill presses can be tricky because if they do not drill 100% vibration-free, they can occasionally crack the bamboo shell or destroy the entire tube.

As I write these lines, I have a wound on my left index finger because I tried to hastily drill a flute in D in the last 20 minutes before our choir rehearsal. In my rush, I did not wear gloves, and of course, the drill slipped off the tube this time!

Before you start drilling, here are some essential tips:

1. **Use a Cordless Drill with High RPM**: Slow drills will cause the bamboo to splinter while drilling, ruining the bamboo tube.
2. **Start with a 7 mm (0.27 in) Drill Bit**: Initially, work with a 7 mm (0.27 in) drill bit. Later, once you have enough experience, you can use 8 or 9 mm (0.31 - 0.35 in) drill bits.
3. **Use High-Quality Wood Drill Bits**: They must be very sharp. Good drill bits have a pointed "centering tip" and sharp "pre-cutters."

Insert a wooden dowel into the bamboo tube to avoid drilling through to the opposite inner side at the beginning. However, I never press the drill against the tube; instead, I press the drill against my hip or stomach and push the tube toward the drill with my left hand. This way, you are less likely to slip. The following annotated images will explain the individual steps of the drilling process:

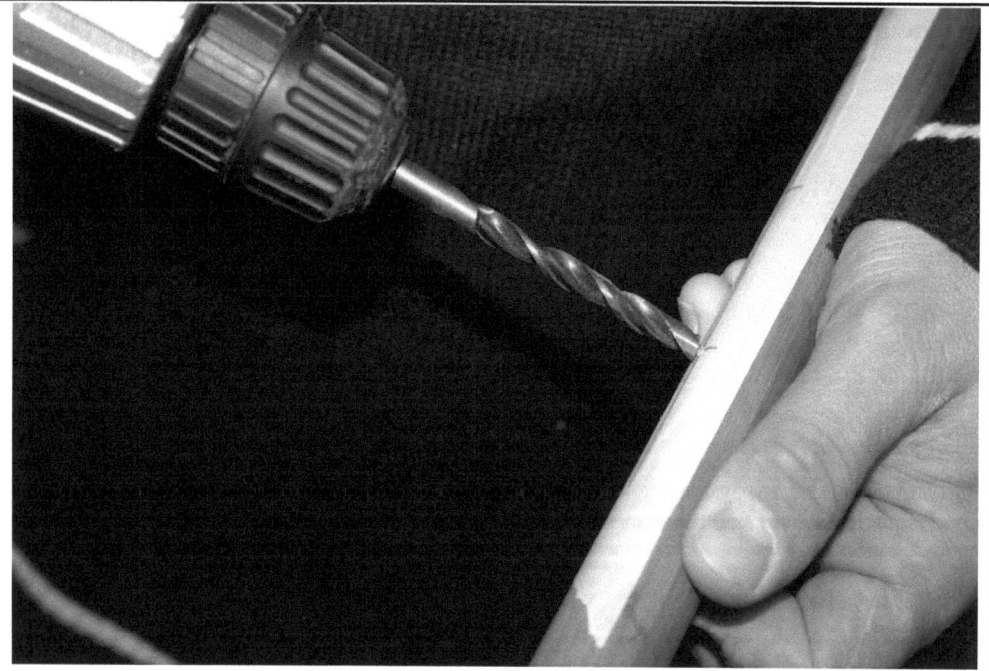

Figure 48: As a right-handed person, I hold the tube in my left hand and the drill in my right. I press the centering tip onto my mark and drill slightly forward, just enough to go about 1 mm deep with the centering tip. This way, the drill won't easily slip off in the second step.

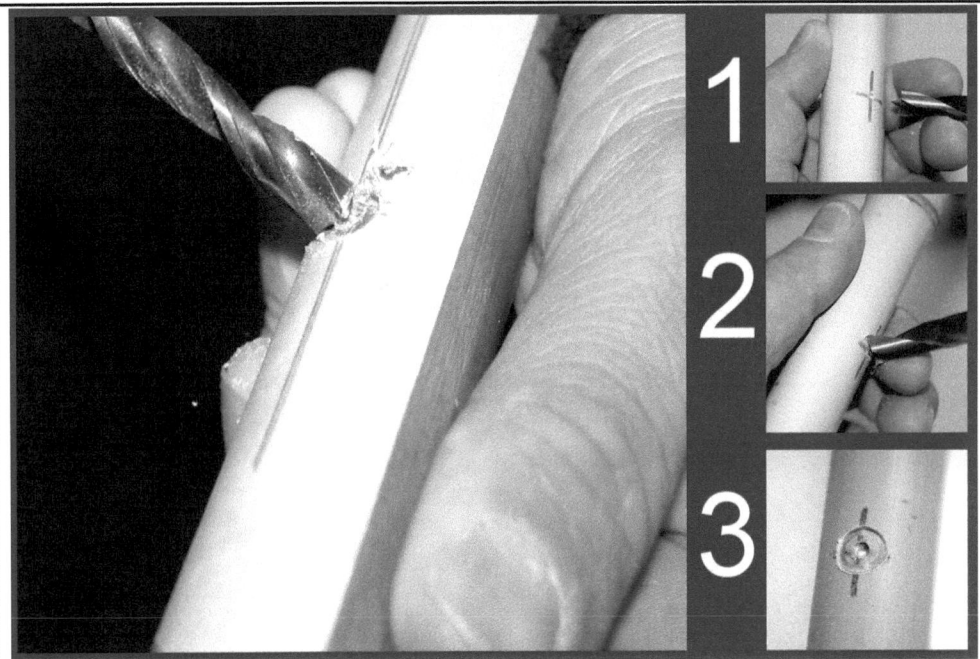

Figure 49:

WARNING: Do not forget the gloves!

In image No. 1, you can see that I have drilled a slight indentation. I have shown it to you without painter's tape so you can better see the effect on the bamboo wood.

In image No. 2, I position the drill so the pre-cutter (edges of the drill bit) contacts the bamboo shell. **Caution:** *Do not drill while your index finger is positioning the drill. I then drill with a circular motion, ensuring that the centering tip remains supported in the center point (1), and the pre-cutters score around the hole's outer edge.*

I drill straight into the tube only when it looks like image No. 3. This prevents the outer shell of the bamboo tube from splintering.

The following image compares an unsuccessful drilling with a successful one.

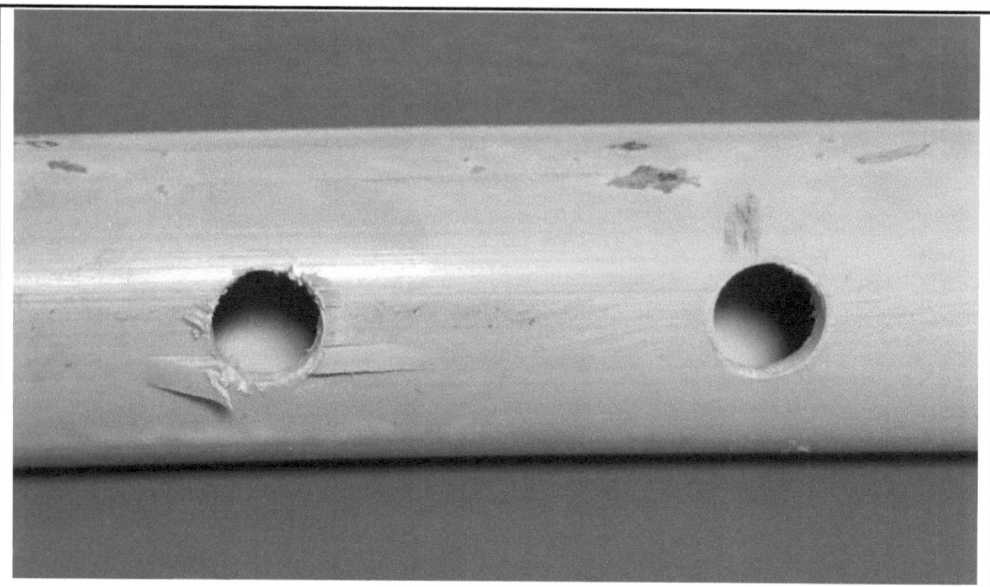

Figure 50: The right hole has precise, smooth edges, while the left hole clearly shows splinters around the edge. In principle, you could sand these down, but often, the splinters extend up to 0.5 cm (0.2 in) around the hole. In such cases, you would need to sand so much that the otherwise beautiful tube shell is completely sanded away at that spot, which does not look very nice.

Perfection needs some practice. If the holes are imperfect the first time, do not let that discourage you. Instead of sanding the splinters away, you can burn them away with a metal rod. I will show you below how to build them on your own. While this leaves a black spot around the hole, it does not look bad after polishing the bamboo flute.

Always drill the lowest hole first. Then, play your flute; if the hole produces the right note, you can drill the next hole. If the first hole produces a much lower note than expected, drilling the next hole one or two millimeters closer to the blowing edge is advisable. Conversely, if the first hole produces the expected note precisely, there is a risk that the next hole will produce a note that is too high. In that case, the second hole should be drilled one or two millimeters closer to the end of the flute. You will learn why this is important in the next section.

Tuning the Finger Holes

Tuning a bamboo flute is not impossible, but it requires a solid knowledge foundation and some experience. If you have measured your flute accurately, there are only five possibilities for how your hole might be tuned:

a. Too high (too sharp)
b. Slightly higher than desired (sharp)
c. Perfectly on note
d. Slightly lower than desired (flat)
e. Too low (too flat)

Assuming you have measured everything correctly and drilled the lowest hole in your Kawala to E major!

Remember you calculated the notes of the E major scale as follows:

E - F# - G# - A - B - C# - D# - E

Without any holes, the Kawala should play a clean E. The note below the first finger hole should be an F#.

Tuning the First Hole F#

As described above, you marked the hole positions and drilled the lowest hole using a 7 mm (0.27 in) drill bit. With a gentle touch, use fine sandpaper to sand the surface and remove any fine splinters.

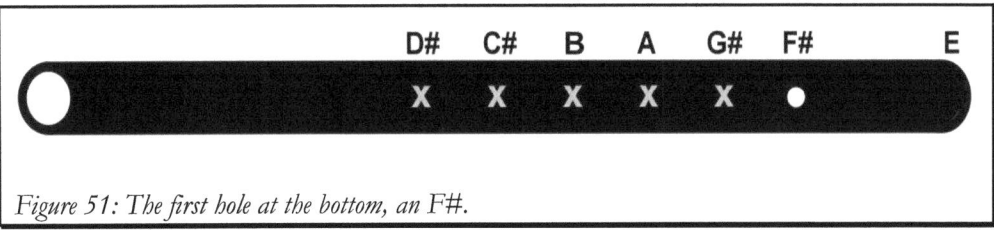

Figure 51: The first hole at the bottom, an F#.

Due to the deliberate choice of a 7 mm (0.27 in) drill bit instead of a 9-10 mm, we should not expect an F# but rather a slightly lower note because the smaller the hole, the lower the note! We deliberately drill the hole with a smaller diameter to force a slightly lower note. After all, it is easier to tune a hole to a higher note than vice versa!

It is high time that we study the most critical factors that determine the pitch of a note. Four factors influence the pitch of a note in a tube with an internal diameter of 18-20 mm (0.70-0.78 in):

1. The position of the drilled hole
2. The diameter of the drilled hole
3. The wall thickness of the flute
4. The angle at which the hole is drilled

This all sounds much more difficult than it is. We simply need to memorize the basic rules for how to raise a note a little, somewhat, much, or significantly much. All we need to remember is to drill the hole somewhat smaller so that the note is slightly lower than expected. To achieve a slightly lower note, you generally do the following:

1. Drill the diameter slightly smaller, e.g., 7 mm (0.27 in) instead of 9 mm
2. After some experience, when you have this intuition that the hole would deliver a higher note, even though all calculations were correct, drill the hole one or one and a half millimeters further away from the blowing edge than initially calculated.

Below, I will graphically present the factors influencing the tuning of the hole. As a beginner, I recommend copying and hanging these on the wall in your workshop or wherever you build your flutes. Such information is essential, distinguishing your flutes from cheap, mistuned ones on the market.

Factor 1: The Distance of the Hole from the Mouthpiece

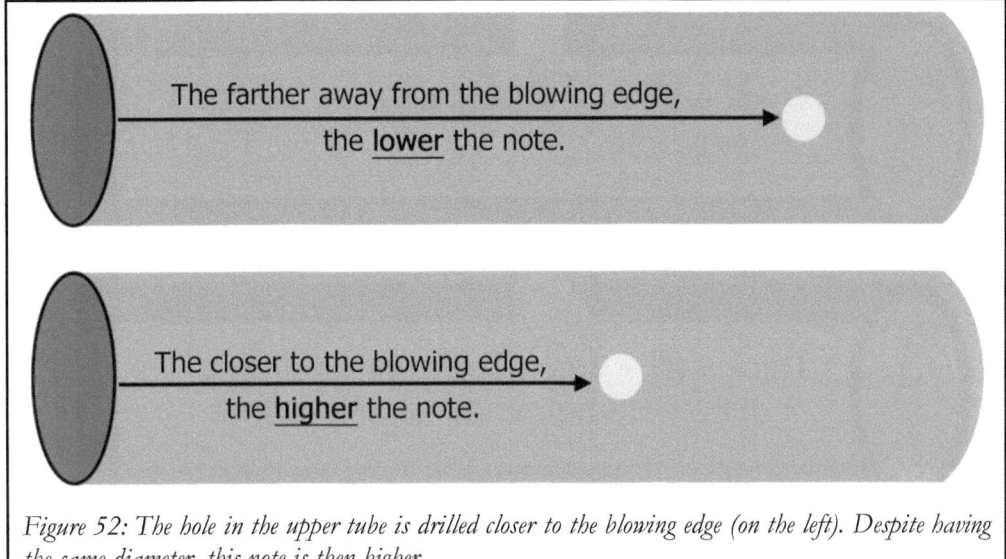

Figure 52: The hole in the upper tube is drilled closer to the blowing edge (on the left). Despite having the same diameter, this note is then higher.

Factor 2: Diameter of the Hole

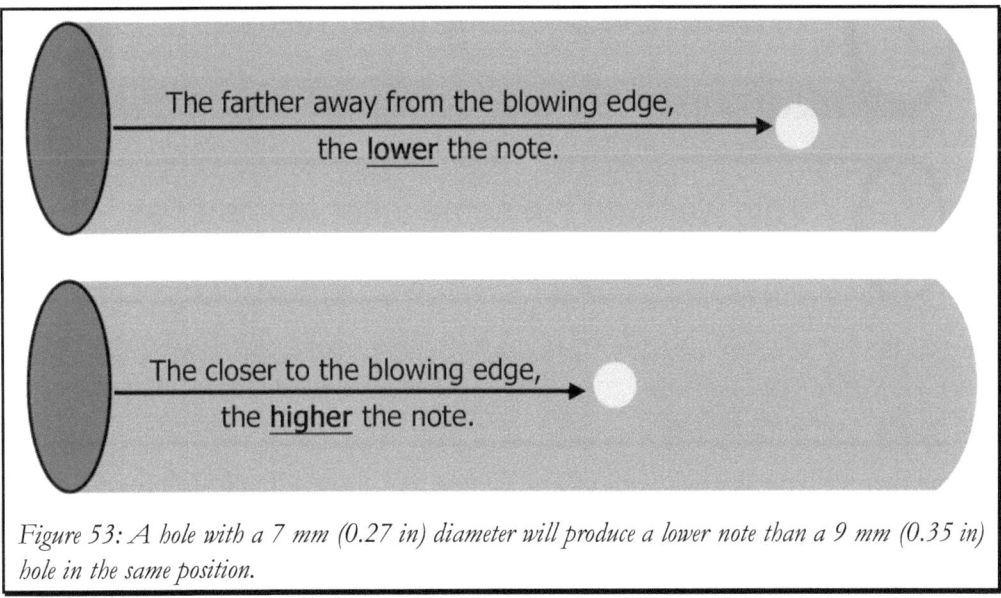

Figure 53: A hole with a 7 mm (0.27 in) diameter will produce a lower note than a 9 mm (0.35 in) hole in the same position.

Factors 3 & 4: Wall Thickness and Drilling Angle

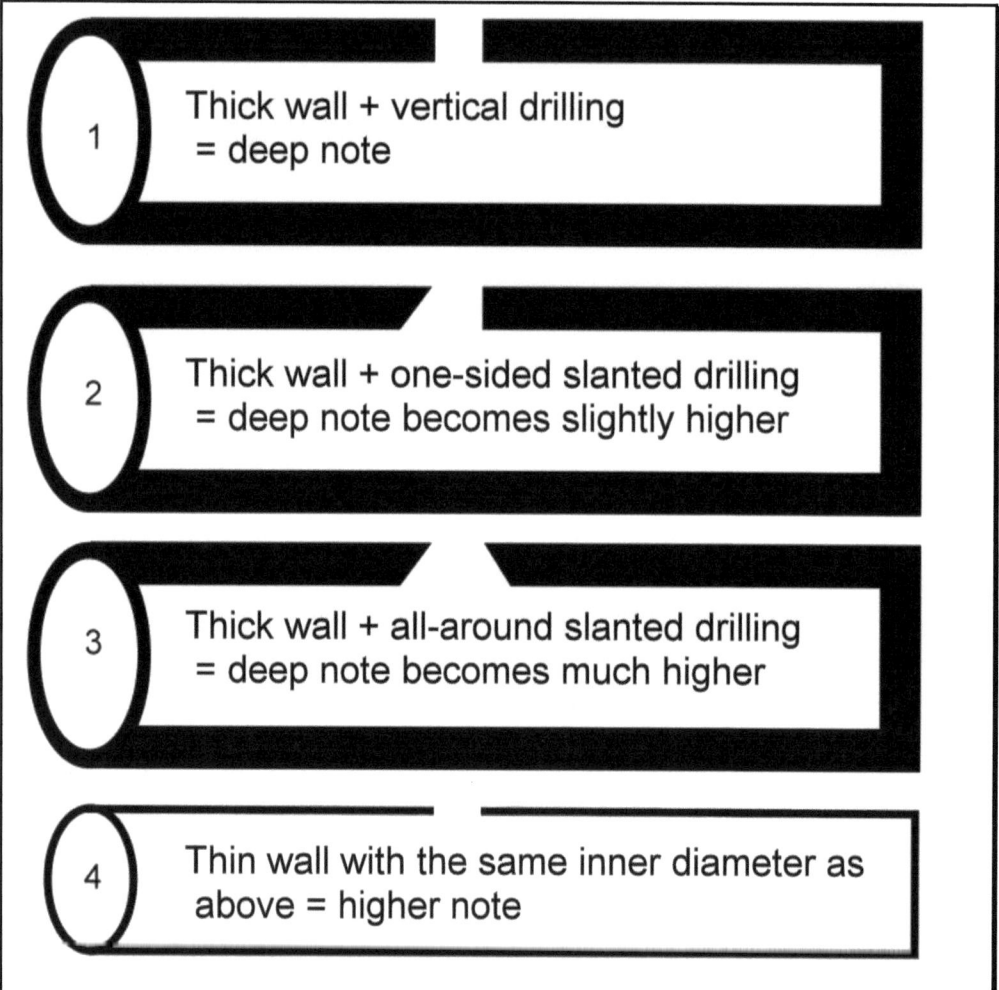

1
Thick wall + vertical drilling
= deep note

2
Thick wall + one-sided slanted drilling
= deep note becomes slightly higher

3
Thick wall + all-around slanted drilling
= deep note becomes much higher

4
Thin wall with the same inner diameter as
above = higher note

Figure 54: The graphic shows three examples with thick-walled bamboo and a fourth with average bamboo thickness. Naturally, rules 1-3 also apply to thin-walled bamboo! However, the influence is so minor that it can hardly be heard.

Now that we have learned about these factors, we should finally drill the F# (P2) hole.

Let us recall our measurements for the hole positions (P 1-6) we calculated above, here together with the expected notes, while the fundamental note is an E:

- H1 = 2 x 3.291 = 6.58 cm (or H1 = 2 x 1.29 = 2.58 in) → Note F#
- H2 = 3 x 3.291 = 9.87 cm (or H2 = 3 x 1.29 = 3.87 in) → Note G#
- H3 = 4 x 3.291 = 13.16 cm (or H3 = 4 x 1.29 = 5.16 in) → Note A
- H4 = 5 x 3.291 = 16.46 cm (or H4 = 5 x 1.29 = 6.45 in) → Note B
- H5 = 6 x 3.291 = 19.75 cm (or H5 = 6 x 1.29 = 7.74 in) → Note C#
- H6 = 7 x 3.291 = 23.04 cm (or H6 = 7 x 1.29 = 9.03 in) → Note D#

Your calculation shows that the F# (Gb) should be drilled at the 6.58 cm (2.58 in) point from the base of your Kawala. In that case, you drill the hole with a 7 mm (0.27 in) drill bit, as previously described, and if everything is correct, you will be at most 50 cents below the desired note when testing your Kawala.

If you are only 10 cents below the F#, you should note that your calculation is exact, and you should drill the second hole 1 mm lower than your calculation suggests. So, drill at position 9.77 cm (3.85 in) instead of 9.87 cm (3,87 in).

We must understand the tuning procedure theoretically before we begin tuning. For this, I want to demonstrate three case examples, assuming you drilled the hole so it is lower than the target note:

1. Approximately 50 cents too low
2. Approximately 25 cents too low
3. Approximately 12.5 cents too low

Be assured that it will work if you understand what you are doing. We will primarily use the first two factors for tuning, specifically the distance of the hole from the mouthpiece and the diameter of the hole. When enlarging a 7 mm (0.27 in) hole to 9 mm (0.31 - 0.35 in), only one of three possibilities can be considered:

1. Enlarging the hole towards the mouthpiece
2. Enlarging the hole evenly, i.e., increase the radius by 1.0 mm to go from a 7 mm (0.27 in) diameter to 9 mm
3. Enlarging the hole towards the foot of the flute

Option 1: Approximately 50 Cents too Low

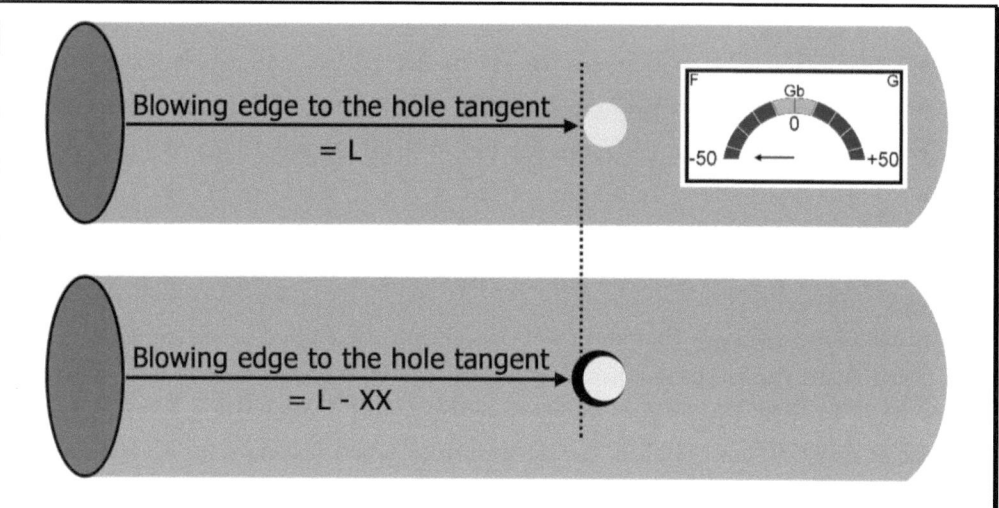

Figure 55: The hole becomes larger, and the distance to the blowing edge is reduced by XX. Therefore, the note becomes significantly higher.

Option 2: Approximately 25 Cents too Low

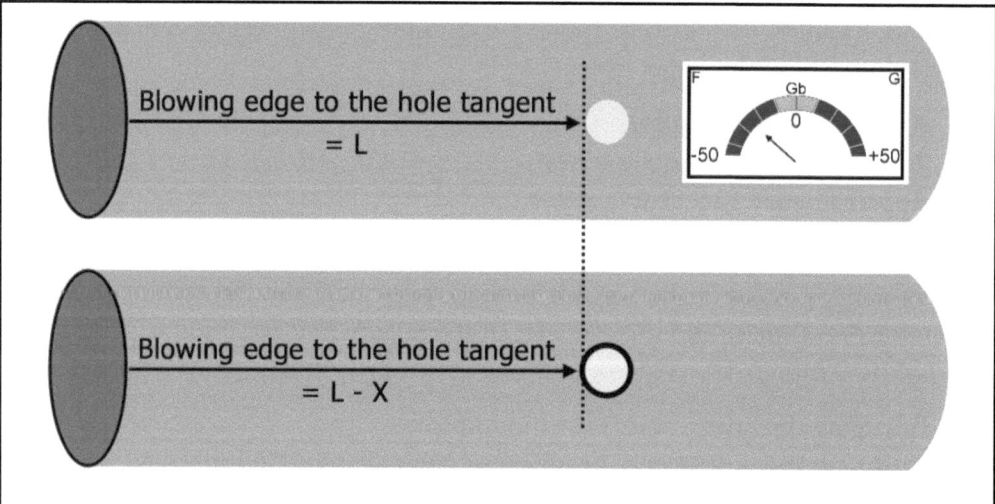

Figure 56: The hole also becomes larger, but the distance to the blowing edge is only slightly reduced by X. Thus, the note becomes somewhat higher.

Option 3: Approximately 12.5 Cents too Low

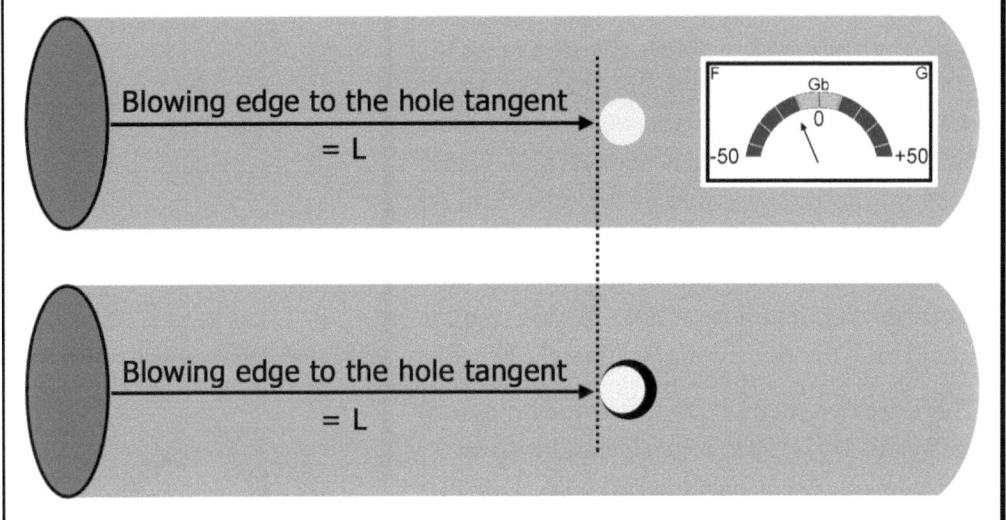

Figure 57: If we enlarge the hole downward towards the flute's foot, we only use the effect that a larger hole slightly raises the note. The distance to the blowing edge remains constant. Thus, the note becomes "slightly" higher.

Fine Adjustment or Fine-Tuning

A hole cannot be made indefinitely larger. 10 - 11 mm (3.92 - 4.33 in) is the maximum size that should be maintained; otherwise, you might have to start plugging your fingers vertically in the holes. What should you do if the note is still slightly too low despite the hole being 10-11 mm (3.92 - 4.33 in)? And what do we do if we have exceeded the measurement and the hole is tuned too high?

Tuning up to 10 cents too high is not unusual. It is the skill of the Kawala player to sway the flute back and forth to "bend" the note into tune. Being over 10 cents is common with Flutes like the Kawala, Salunag, Anasazi, Shakuhachi, Bansuri, Dizi, and Ney. But in modern times, it is more of a hindrance when we want to play with Western standardized instruments. Therefore, we need to find a way to tune the flute a little higher, even though our hole is already 11 mm in diameter, and, of course, also find a way to tune a slightly too high hole lower.

Fine-Tuning Case 1: The Note is Still Slightly Too Low

If the note is still slightly too low, you can enlarge the hole slightly from the inside of the tube. On the right (Figure 58), you see a split tube with images from the inner side of the holes. Both holes have a diameter of 9 mm (3,54 in) on the outer side of the tube. You do not need to burn around the entire hole from the inside immediately; do it step by step until the note fits. The lower hole in this graphic would raise the note by approximately 20 cents.

There are two methods to widen the hole from the inside. If you have a steady hand with burning, you can use a burning rod with a smaller diameter to burn it as if you were hollowing out a tomato. There, you also have a smaller hole, and you scrape out the flesh with circular movements. The more professional method is to create a special burning rod for this purpose. How to do this is explained below under "Making your Buring Rods" in a couple of pages.

Figure 58: Inner view of holes.

Fine-Tuning Case 2: The Note is Slightly Too High

I rarely mistune my notes too high, but customers often send in mistuned flutes for repair. For holes that are too high (sharp), I use the grain method, attaching a rice or lentil-sized obstacle to the inner wall above the affected hole. I create the "grain" from wood putty and glue. I apply glue to the spot with a cotton swab, then press the "grain" into place using a homemade spoon. I position the flute with holes facing down on the workbench, supporting it to prevent rolling, and leave it for an hour or two.

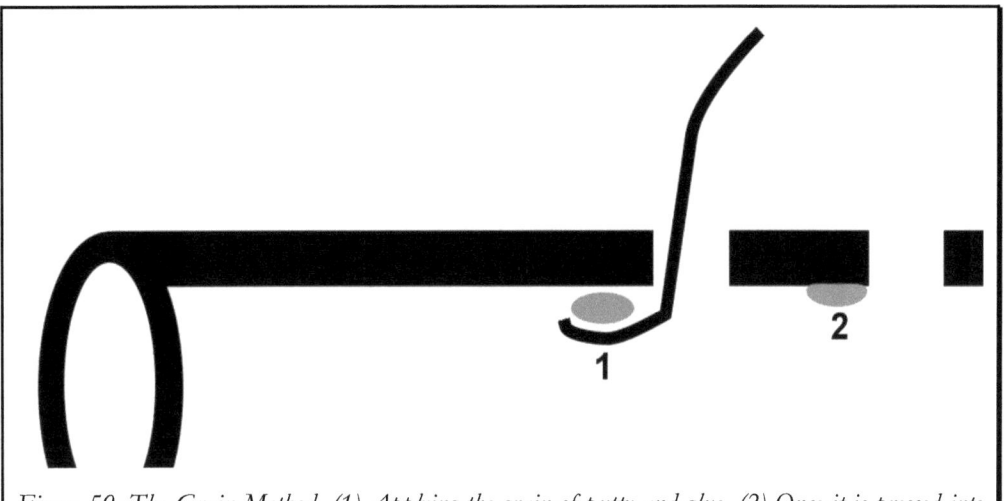

Figure 59: The Grain Method. (1) Applying the grain of putty and glue. (2) Once it is pressed into place.

Figure 60: You can find a suitable tool for applying the soft grain in an inexpensive wood carving set. You can bend the tip to have a spoon, as in Figure 59.

Making your Burning Rods

Before you begin tuning your flute, you need the necessary tools. I tune my flutes by adjusting the holes with burning rods.

Some years ago, I discovered online that you could import such rods. I paid about 100 euros and had to wait a long time. A wooden handle and a wood drill bit cost you about 10 euros and will do fine.

However, you would also need a bench grinder!

If you do not intend to build dozens of flutes, ask your car mechanic if you could use his bench grinder. However, nothing is easier than making a burning rod.

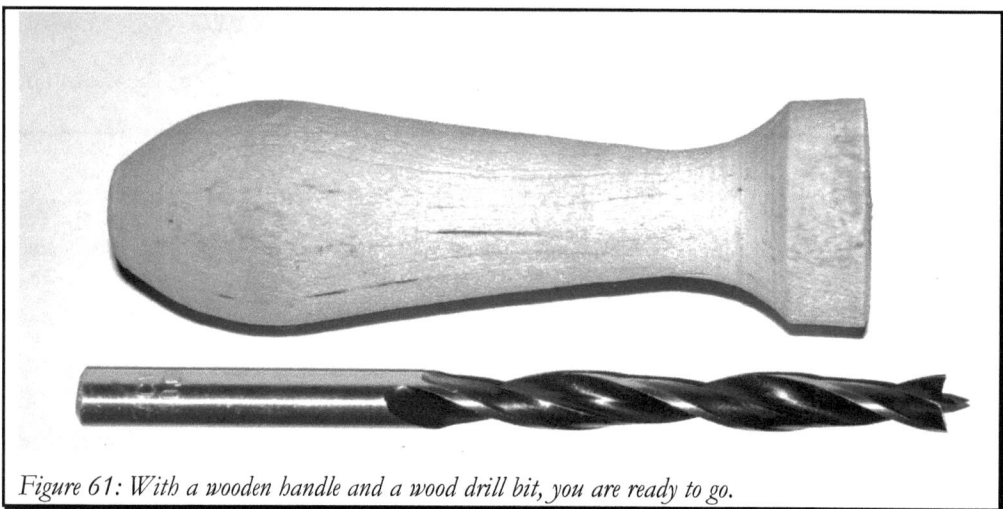

Figure 61: With a wooden handle and a wood drill bit, you are ready to go.

Drill your drill bit halfway into the wooden handle.

Now you need the bench grinder. I got mine from the hardware store for about 40 euros. I just checked on eBay Germany and found the cheapest new "double grinder" for 22,99 euros (free shipping). Such a tool is a good investment if you have a small workshop in your house or flat.

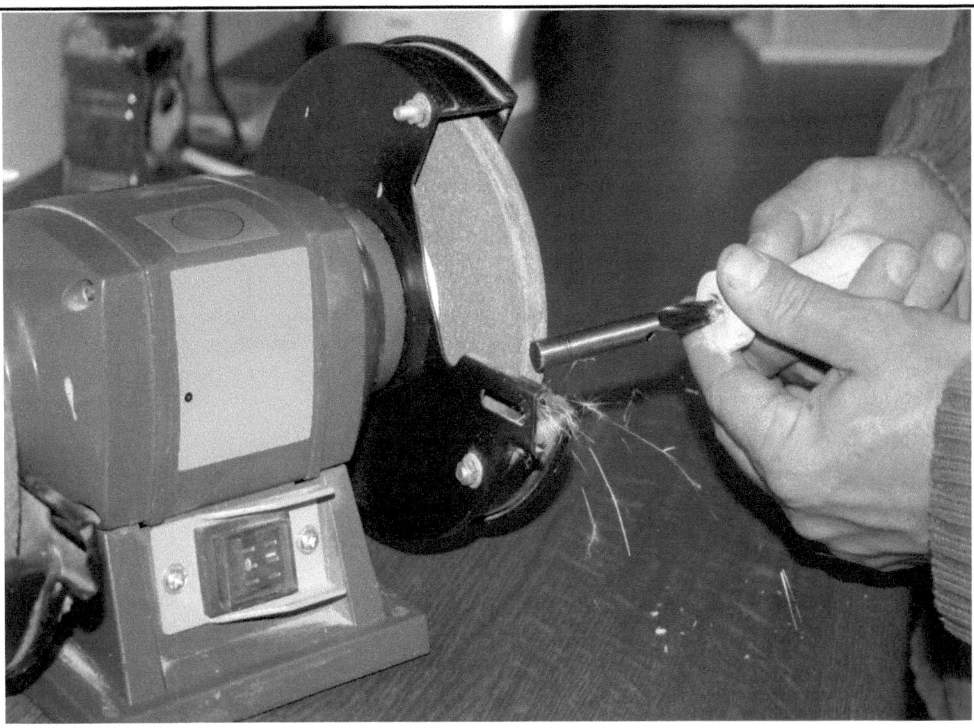

Figure 63: I am grinding the tip of my newly built burning rod so that it becomes like a blunt pencil.

Remember that grinding generates many sparks, and you should first remove wood dust from your workshop to avoid fire hazards. I always feel uneasy about these things, so I grind on a tiled floor, ensuring nothing nearby can catch fire.

On the right in the image, you can see how the 10 mm (3.93 in) tip has been ground down to approximately an 8 mm (3.14 in) tip.

Figure 62: The tip of the burning rod.

I have been working with a maximum of two burning rods for years. However, I have attached a wood drill bit to both sides of the handle. This way, the burning rod does not fall forward when I lay it on a block for heating, as shown in the picture below.

Figure 64: I have inserted two screws into the wooden block here; you can only see one of the screws. The screws ensure that the burning rod does not roll to the side.

This burning rod, for instance, has two different ends. The side glowing in the fire in the image is 10 mm (3,93701)and tapers to 5 mm (1,9685) at the tip. The other side (see picture on the right) is designed to burn the tube from the inside out. For this, you need to skillfully grind the end so that it has a wider tip. With a bench grinder, such a construction can be com-

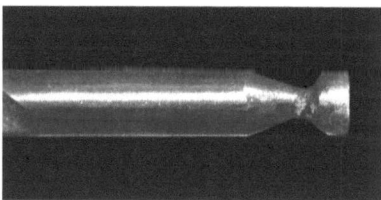

Figure 65: Burning rod for burning the tube from the inside.

pleted within 10 minutes. Be careful not to make the narrowest part too thin.

Safety Note (1)

Keep an old pot of water nearby when tuning. After burning, the rod may transfer enough heat to the wooden handle to pose a fire hazard. Always extinguish burning rods after tuning!

And another note:

Safety Note (2)

Burning bamboo creates much smoke, harming your respiratory system and mucous membranes. Always work outdoors or in well-ventilated areas. I devised a DIY solution to replace face masks when testing flutes. I cut a kitchen sponge into small pieces to fit snugly in my nostrils, moisten them, and insert them. Though it looks odd, it effectively blocks smoke when the extractor fan does not fully clear it. If you do it also, then at your own risk!

Burning the Holes:

Now, we need to put all the theories about tuning into practice. It is straightforward as long as you have studied the rules. Play your Kawala and check how much higher you need to tune a hole. When enlarging the hole by burning, you can choose one of the three options below, depending on how you need to tune your flute.

Using the example in the graphic on the right, if the blowing edge is on the left, I would tune the holes:

1. 50 cents higher,
2. 25 cents higher, and
3. 12.5 cents higher

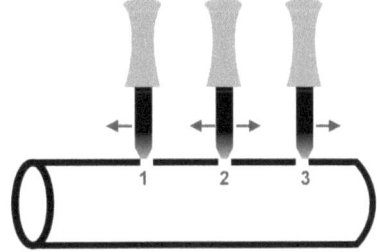

Figure 66: Tuning with a burning rod

73

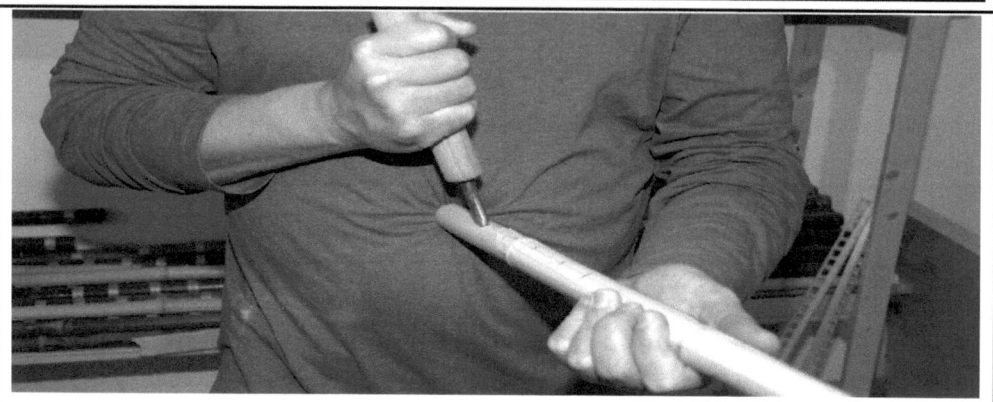

Figure 67: Here, I want to tune the last hole according to Rule No. 3. I press the flute's foot against my stomach and burn the hole by pulling the burning rod toward my stomach as I press it in. However, I do this only until the hole has a diameter of 10 mm (0.39 in).

Do not try to drill and burn all the holes simultaneously, especially if you have little experience. You begin drilling and burning the second hole after you have tuned your first (lowest) hole. After a couple of flutes, you will have enough experience to drill all the holes and then do the tuning.

There is a good reason for this: the more holes in a row below the note being tuned, the higher the note of that particular hole will be.

Let me explain this with a few pictures:

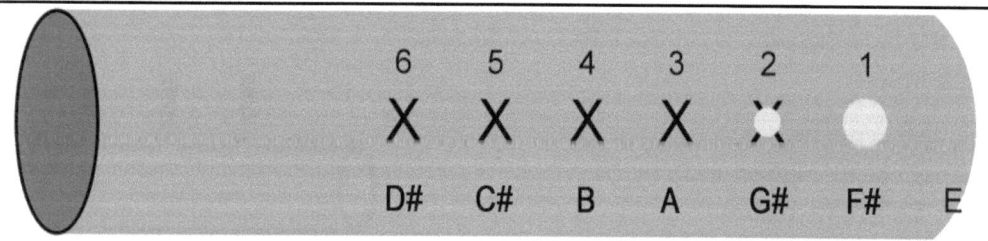

Figure 68: Here, we have already drilled our first hole, the F#, and tuned it appropriately. If we drill the G# with a 7 mm (0.27 in) bit, it will probably be 5-15 cents too low.

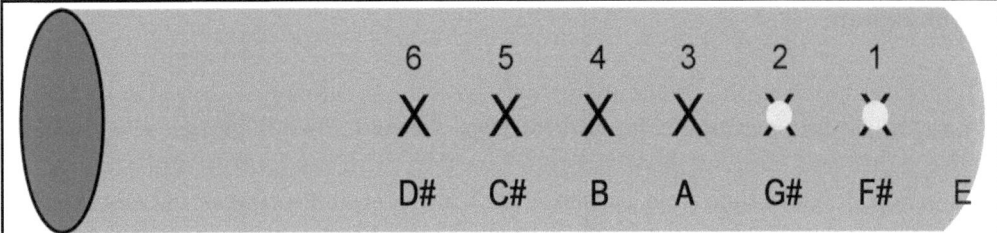

Figure 69: Here, we assume that you have drilled both holes with a 7 mm (0.27 in) bit, planning to do the fine-tuning in one go. This time, the G# indicates it is 20-30 cents too low because the F# hole is not yet large enough, allowing less air to escape. There is a risk that you might drill the A hole slightly higher to avoid having it too low as well.

The Misinterpretation!

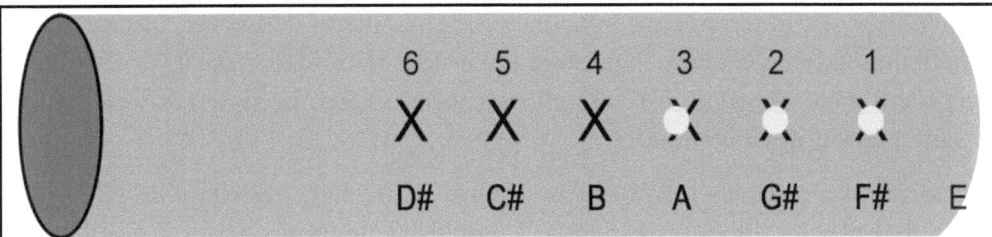

Figure 70: Here, it has happened. You drilled the A slightly higher to be only 10 cents lower instead of 30 cents lower.

The Result of the Error

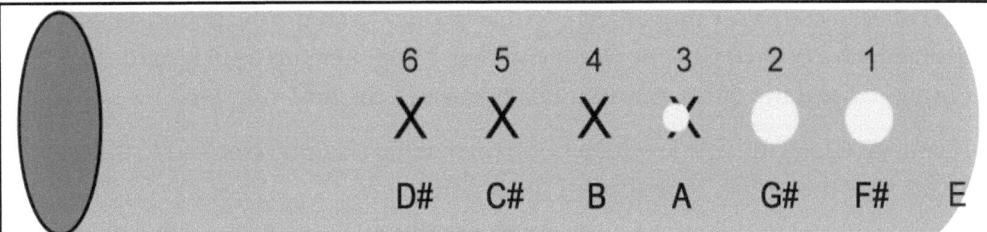

Figure 71: When you play the A after fine-tuning holes 1 and 2, you will probably find it already in tune or possibly too high. Because of the large holes 1 and 2, the air escapes more quickly compared to Figure 70, making the note A slightly higher than desired!

Conclusion:

The note's pitch is not determined solely by the individual hole but also by how many holes are open below it and how large they are. As a beginner, you should always drill and tune one hole at a time, starting from the bottom and moving up—first drill and tune hole 1, then hole 2, and so on. Soon, you will develop an eye for this and be able to drill all the holes first while keeping these nuances in mind.

The Internal Treatment of the Flute

Bamboo is a type of wood that naturally absorbs moisture. It can crack, especially when exposed to temperature fluctuations while damp. However, utterly dried-out bamboo can also crack. Therefore, we need a method to make it largely water-repellent while allowing just enough moisture to keep the flute functioning for many years, if not a lifetime.

Traditionally, and even today, bamboo flutes are treated internally with oil. When I started playing the Ney as a child, I would fill the flutes with oil every other month and let them drain in the sink, which naturally had its consequences.

When I eventually began building flutes, I started coating the inner walls with oil, using a stocking on a wooden stick to control the amount of oil.

Many years later, after moving to Germany, I discovered solvent-free acrylic lacquer, which I poured into my flutes and then hung them up until it hardened. But this would seal the flutes entirely, which was not the best solution.

If you have read my first German book on making bamboo transverse flutes, you might remember this. Nowadays, I do it differently.

Below are some detailed pictures to follow each step I take.

You will need the following:

- A rod made of copper or wood
- A long stocking or a homemade fabric bag
- A brush
- Solvent-free wood glue or acrylic lacquer (for instance, solvent-free acrylic lacquer for parquet floors at a hardware store)
- Painter's masking tape
- Shellac (see below)
- A measuring cup
- A mat to protect your table or floor
- Cotton swabs (or a small sharp carving knife)

Step 1: The Acrylic or Wood Glue Primer

Figure 72: I am inserting a copper pipe (diameter = 12 mm / 0.47 in) into an old fabric flute case. I have also been buying cheap, thin socks from Amazon, which I have used for this purpose for several years.

Figure 73: Now, apply a small amount of acrylic lacquer or wood glue (without solvents) to the bag. Just enough to make it slightly damp.

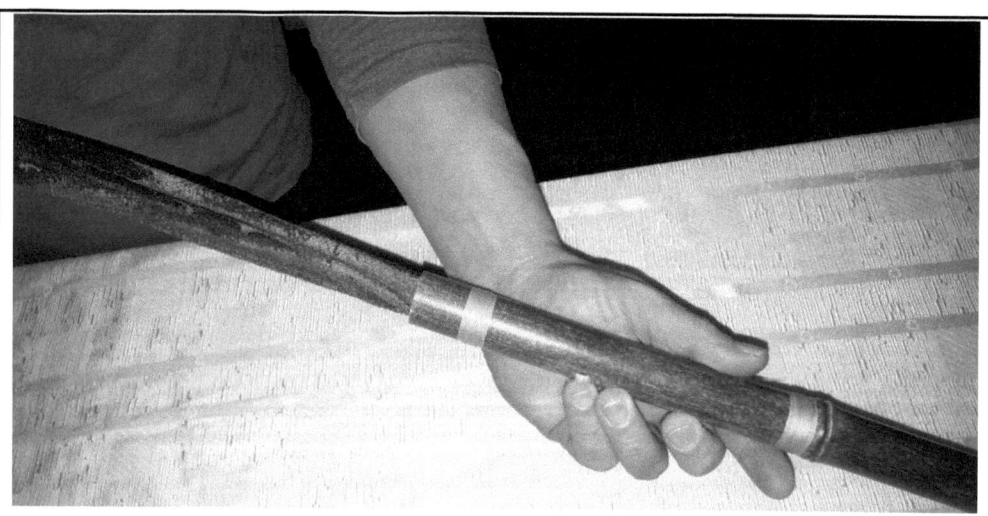

Figure 74: Slide the rod in and out of the flute several times. With a few deft twists, all the bamboo dust will stick to the bag. Wash the bag immediately; otherwise, the lacquer or glue will harden, and you will not be able to use it again. If you are making multiple flutes and want to save socks, I recommend using the rod with the sock to remove the dust from all the flutes before doing it with acrylic or glue.

As often happens, acrylic lacquer or wood glue drips accumulate in the finger holes (see image on the right).

You need to remove this as quickly as possible. While cotton swabs can work, it is even better to sharpen a carving knife to easily remove or scrape off the excess.

You can then wipe the carving knife clean and reuse it repeatedly, unlike the cotton swabs.

Figure 75: Remove the drips from the holes.

You can stand the flute upright after removing the acrylic or wood glue drips. I usually lean the flutes against the wall for this. Also, be aware that varnish often collects at the ends of the flute. Wipe it off quickly with a cloth before it hardens.

If you have not used too much material but only as much to coat the inside walls lightly, the flute will dry in 30 minutes, though I always

Figure 76: Scraping off the drips.

prefer to wait an hour or two before proceeding with the inner shellac coating.

Step 2: Preparing Shellac

If you are already familiar with shellac, you can skip this step.

The resin known as shellac is derived from the secretions of the female lac bug, native to the forests of India and Thailand. After being collected, the resin is processed into dry flakes, which can be dissolved in alcohol to form a versatile liquid for wood finishing and food glazing.

It is non-toxic, biodegradable, and moisture-resistant. However, it is not water-proof, which we will use to our advantage.

You can purchase ready-made shellac polish. I recommend the pale blonde shellac polish if you prefer to buy ready-made shellac. However, it is best to prepare your shellac polish. You can then make thick and thin shellac and determine its consistency yourself.

You can find shellac flakes online in various shops, especially those specializing in restoration and wood treatment. Pale blonde shellac is ideal for bamboo, though many other colors are available. You will also need pure alcohol. I use bioethanol and bio-shellac flakes when preparing my shellac lacquer.

Figure 77: Shellack flakes, that will be desolved in alcohol

For the polish, I mix about one part shellac with two parts alcohol. I mix the shellac and alcohol in a 1:1 ratio for thicker shellac suitable for the interior walls of my flutes.

The simplest method is to fill a plastic bottle two-thirds full with shellac flakes and then fill the bottle with alcohol just below the neck. Lay the bottle on its side and shake it every few hours until the shellac is completely dissolved. This process can ruin your weekend, but it is undoubtedly worthwhile. If you want to speed up the process, you can put the shellac flakes into a blender to have shellac dust (or sand). It will help dissolve it comparatively fast in alcohol.

Next, pour half of the mixture into another bottle, which you fill with alcohol up to three-quarters full. The first bottle contains the thick shellac for the inside of the flutes, while the second bottle holds the shellac for the exterior polish, which I will explain to you shortly. If the thick shellac seems too thick, add some alcohol. These two bottles will last for 50 flutes or more. Nevertheless, after using them for a couple of weeks, you will notice that the shellac is getting thicker because alcohol evaporates quickly. However, you will have gained the necessary experience to add a suitable amount of alcohol to each of your bottles to achieve the required thickness.

One kilogram of shellac costs approximately 20-30 euros. Two liters of denatured alcohol are also quite affordable, allowing you to produce about 2.5 liters of homemade shellac for just a few euros.

Step 3: Treating the Inner Wall with Shellac

First, it is important to remember that shellac is not entirely waterproof, as it swells when exposed to water. I have often been asked why shellac is used on the inner wall of the flute and whether it will swell. I always respond, "Our mouth is not a water faucet." The slight humidity introduced into the flute through our breath is not the same as submerging shellac in a water bowl. In my experience, this property, which is not fully waterproof, helps make the flute somewhat breathable while protecting the wood. After playing, you should always stand the flute upright, for example, by leaning it against a wall so that any excess moisture can escape.

The humidity from the breath is not a problem unless excessive moisture enters the wood, especially when combined with temperature fluctuations. A little residual moisture is even desirable.

After 44 years of building bamboo flutes, I am convinced that the best protection for them is a combination of pre-treatment with acrylic lacquer or wood glue and finally with shellac. Many instruments, especially string instruments and pianos, are coated with shellac. I have never seen an instrument's body disintegrate just because of sweat on a musician's hands. However, it would be best not to place a wet glass of water on a shellac-treated surface, which will cause water stains.

Furthermore, a shellac finish greatly enhances the sound of the flute. Throughout my life, I have likely built thousands of flutes. I have experimented with various oils, polishes, lacquers, acrylics, and other sealants, but none compare to this dual treatment. First, acrylic lacquer or wood glue is applied minimally using a rod with a bag or sock (refer to figures 71-73) so as not to seal the entire inner wall of the flute. Where the acrylic varnish or wood glue has not sealed the inside of the flute, and should not, the shellac in the second part of the treatment will penetrate the wood pores of the bamboo and form "roots" to securely hold the entire shellac layer. This process allows moisture from your breath to enter the bamboo on a minimal "molecular" level, ensuring that the bamboo tube stays "alive" and does not dry out.

If you know or discover a better method, I am all ears!

Of course, you could use a varnish that completely seals the flute and makes it as waterproof as a glass pane. In that case, you might as well make your flute from a copper or aluminum tube, which does not sound so bad! However, the warm bamboo sound comes only from a bamboo tube where the structure has not been completely altered.

Filling the Flute with Shellac and Letting it Drain

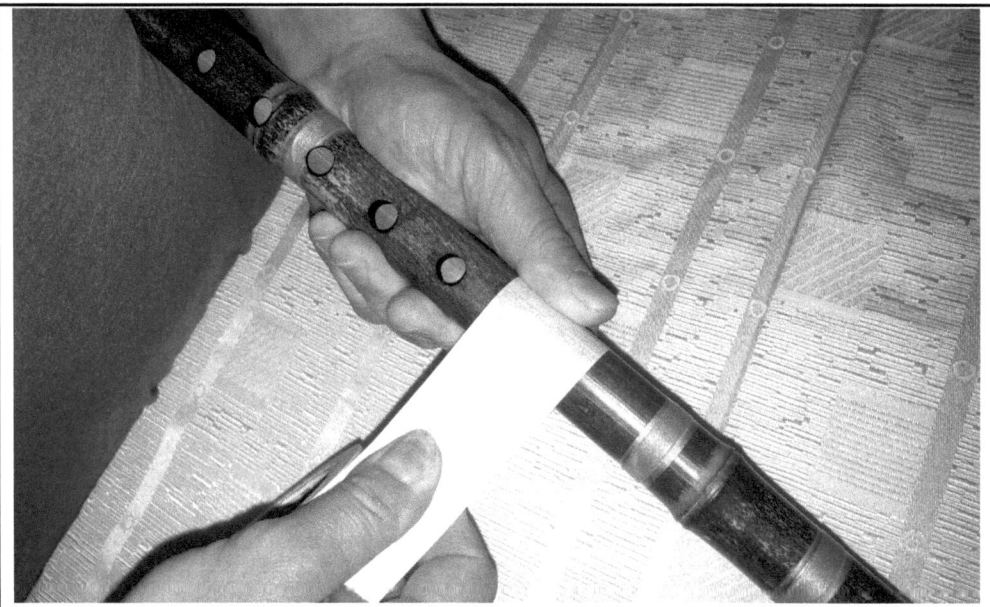

Figure 78: First, close all six holes and ensure that you have no gaps under the painter's tape at the holes. You can press the tape firmly around the holes with your thumb. If the tape is not securely attached, you could end up with a terrible mess later. The actual secret lies in buying a high-quality painter's tape. Sparing money here is something you will regret.

I press the flute end (foot) into my left hand's palm as a right-hander. In the past, I also used to close the foot with painter's tape. However, the tape often came loose under the weight of the shellac once the flute was filled with it. And if you are unlucky, everything ends up on the floor. Before pouring in your shellac, try to blow into the flute. Where air escapes, shellac will naturally escape as well. Sure, you can try using a cork, but in my experience, doing it by hand is the fastest and cleanest way to achieve the final result. A cork would, for instance, prevent the shellac from reaching the very bottom end.

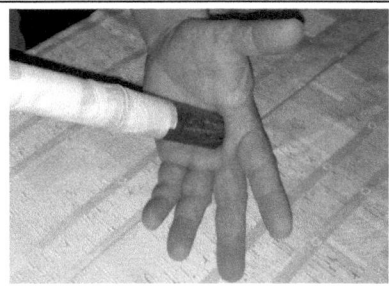

Figure 79: Closing the end of the flute with the eft hand.

I close my left hand and hold the flute very firmly. To prevent the flute from wobbling, I press my forearm against my hip and, as unfortunately visible in the picture, lean the flute against my stomach.

In the next step, I carefully pour the shellac into the flute from the top.

If you have done everything correctly, no shellac will leak from the holes under the tape, nor from the bottom end where you are holding the flute tightly.

My biggest mistake is that I sometimes get distracted and pour too much shellac. This still happens occasionally, even after all these years.

Filling two-thirds of the flute is entirely sufficient. If you concentrate, you will feel the pressure of the shellac in the flute. It feels like the flute wants to tip over, which is a clear sign

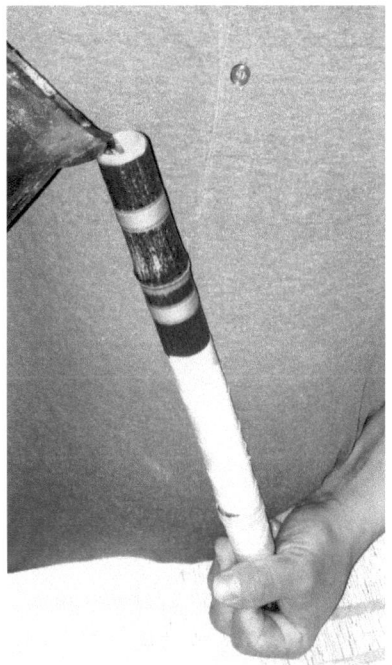

Figure 80: Filling the pipe with shellac

to stop pouring. If you position the flute to see the covered holes while pouring in your shellac, you will notice how it reaches one hole after the other, indicating when to stop.

Then, I place my measuring cup next to the flute and lift my left hand, allowing the shellac to flow out slowly. As it flows, I rotate the flute along its longitudinal axis so that the entire inner surface gets coated with shellac. Only at the end do I hold the flute upright to let it drain.

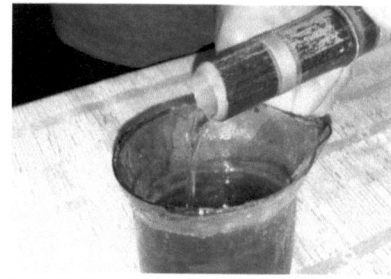

Figure 81: Puring out the Shellac.

When inspecting your flute, ensure all areas are coated with shellac. Do not put your eye too close to the flute, as shellac in the eye is unpleasant. Speed is crucial as shellac dries quickly. The liquid is alcohol with shellac flakes, which evaporates, leaving a shellac film.

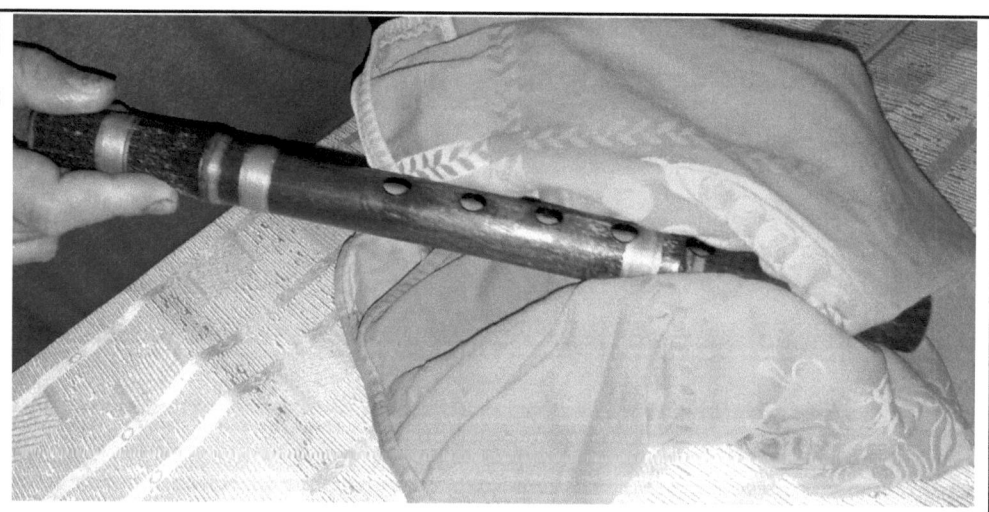

Figure 82: After I remove the painter's tape, I quickly wipe the flute with a towel to remove any shellac that has collected under the tape. There are usually a few drops on the blowing edge as well. You should wipe away these drops, too.

You need to work quickly and place your flute somewhere to allow the shellac on the inner wall to dry. If you want to apply a second coat of shellac, you should do so only after 15 minutes for the second coating and 20-30 minutes for a third coating so the previous coating is hard enough not to be dissolved by the alcohol in the following application. However, you should not wait too long, as it is better if the first coat has not fully cured. This allows the shellac film from the second application to bond better with the first.

You can test the flute after just an hour, but only briefly. It should be fully used after a couple of days and completely hardened after 10-14 days.

The Exterior Treatment of the Flute

For an excellent exterior treatment, you will need the following materials:

- Good quality cotton yarn (about 1 mm thick and, most importantly, not too fuzzy)
- A sharp knife or a cutter from your office
- A kitchen sponge
- Scissors
- The second shellac, which you have prepared or purchased (shellac polish)

Binding Bamboo Flutes

Binding the bamboo flutes, not only Kawalas, primarily protects it. The principle is quite simple: tightly binding the flute with cotton or other plant-based yarn becomes less prone to cracking. Even if a crack eventually occurs, the strong bindings will ensure it does not spread and will not affect the flute's functionality.

Among the many bamboo flutes I have restored, even the most expensive Japanese shakuhachis were sent in for repair after developing cracks. Good bindings can save you the cost of an expensive restoration!

The binding should generally be done before applying the exterior lacquer. Since the binding is made from cotton or other natural yarns (like linen or hemp twine), it will absorb the shellac during lacquering and become slightly thicker. This causes the binding to grip the bamboo more tightly, offering additional protection. However, there are ways to make it even more robust, which we will discuss below.

I will now demonstrate the binding process step by step. You can bind with double yarn, wrapping two threads simultaneously, or with a thicker yarn. I recently preferred using the "Catania" cotton yarn (50g) from "Schachenmayr." Its thickness is suitable for single binding. Another option is to use yarn from the company Aida, size 5. I fold two threads together with this yarn to make a double yarn. In the explanatory images below, I use a double garn in some pictures; in others, I do not.

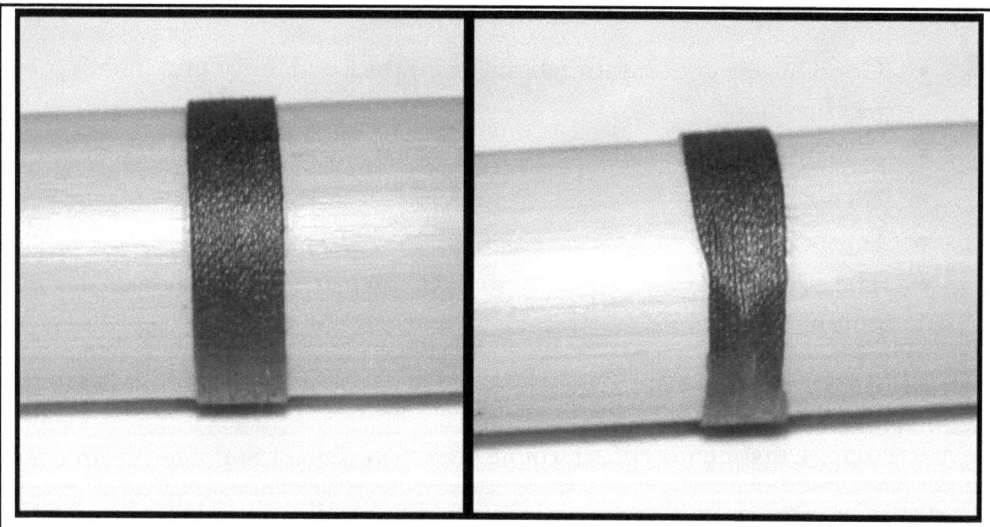

Figure 83: This is our goal: on the left, the binding at the front, and on the right, the binding at the back, where a knot is tied under the binding to ensure it stays tight and firm.

In the following section, I will explain the binding process first with six graphics, followed by several detailed images so you can follow each step.

It is important not to lose patience in this process. You just need to practice. Everything can be learned, but experience must be gained. When my son turned 15, he started learning how to bind flutes. It took him a week to master it. So, do not give up! I suggest the following:

- First, read the following two sections: the one with the explanatory graphics and the one with the explanatory photos, where I demonstrate the binding.
- After that, simply take some yarn and a tube no longer than 50 cm (19.68 in) and practice!

A Binding in Six Steps

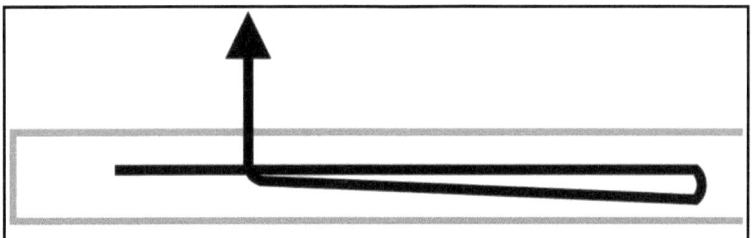

Figure 84: Place the yarn on the flute from left to right. Then, bring the thread back to create a loop.

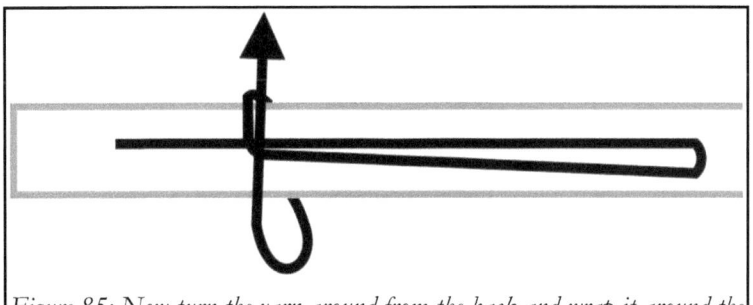

Figure 85: Now turn the yarn around from the back and wrap it around the flute.

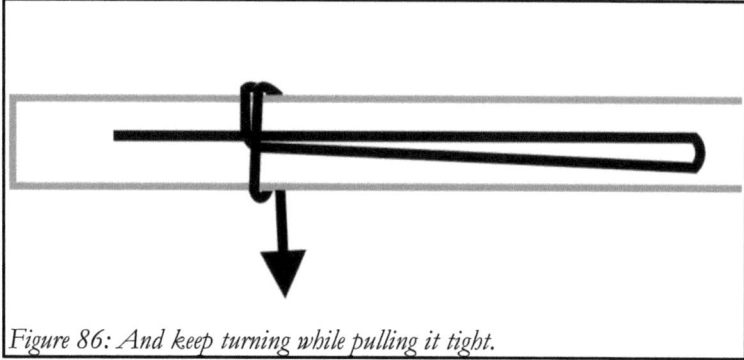

Figure 86: And keep turning while pulling it tight.

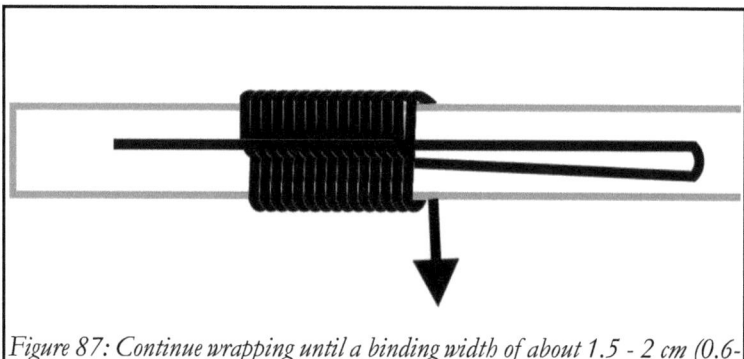

Figure 87: Continue wrapping until a binding width of about 1.5 - 2 cm (0.6-0.8 in).

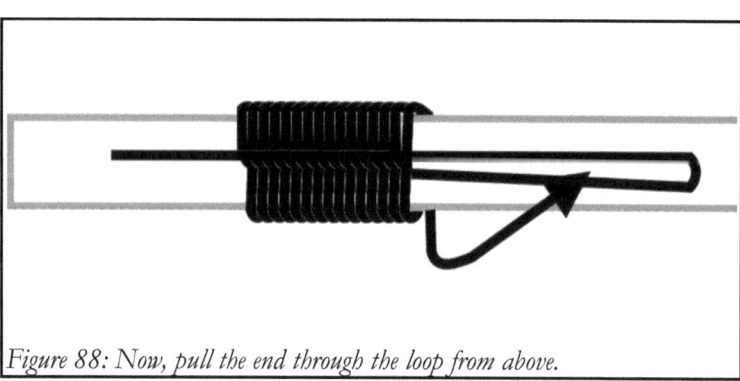

Figure 88: Now, pull the end through the loop from above.

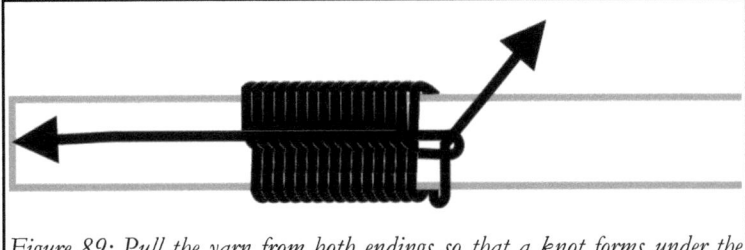

Figure 89: Pull the yarn from both endings so that a knot forms under the binding.

To make it as understandable as possible, here is how I actually make a binding. You might decide to use different fingers to keep the yarn taut, but I strongly recommend copying my method until you get the hang of it.

Detailed Images for Binding

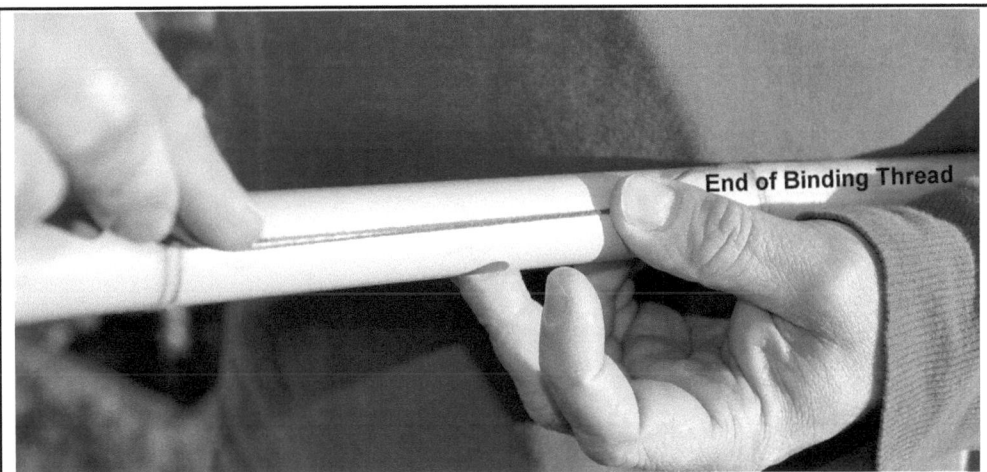

Figure 90: I press down on the taut yarn with my left thumb, leaving about a 5 cm overhang at the end (the right side of the image).

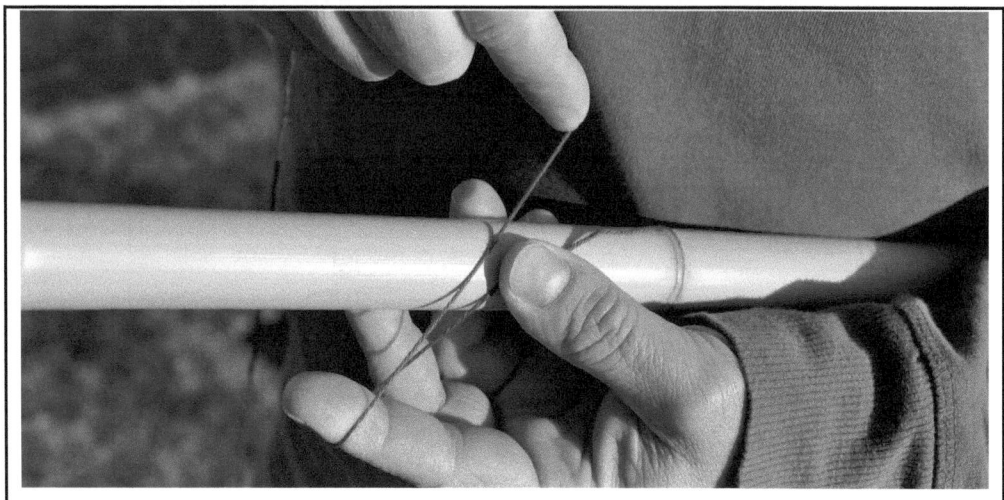

Figure 91: With my right hand, I pull the yarn over the tip of my left index finger.

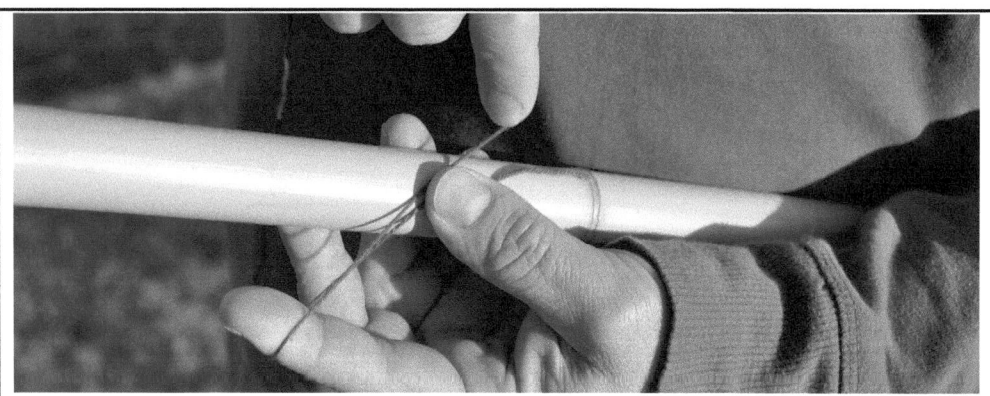

Figure 92: I pull the yarn to hold it under my left thumb. Notice that I use a single yarn here compared to the following image.

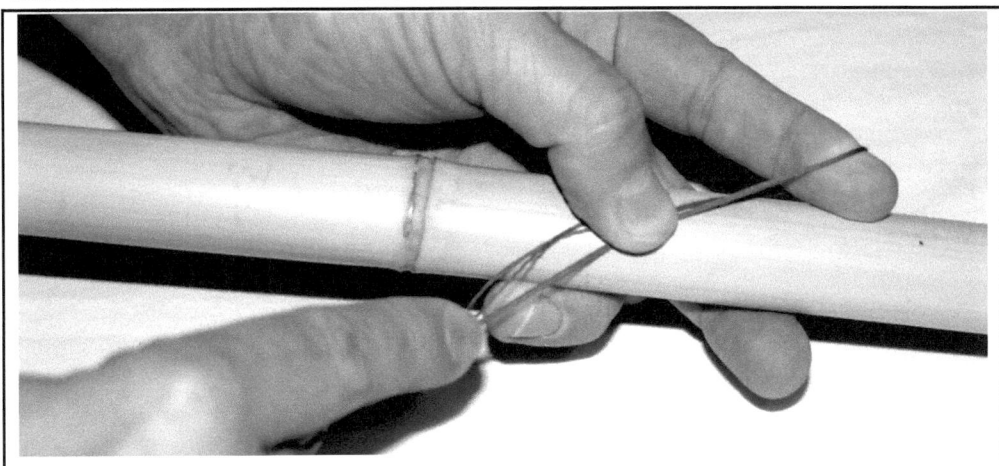

Figure 93: Just another image showing the previous illustration from a different perspective. Make sure to keep your index finger tight, as it forms the loop that will bind the entire wrapping later. If you compare this image with the previous ones, you may notice that I am using here a double yarn.

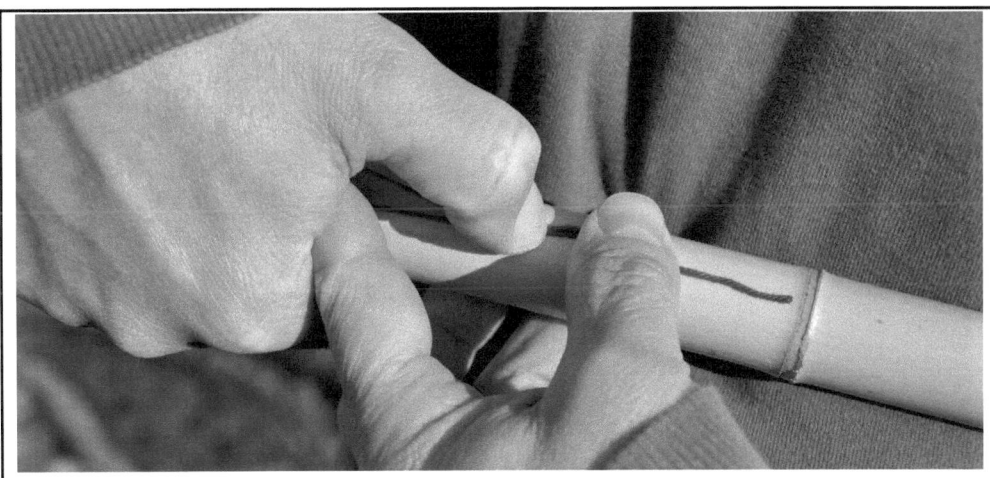

Figure 94: This is possibly a difficult step, but with some training, you will manage to do it also. I grasp the yarn with my right thumbnail and press it firmly. I am preparing to reposition my left hand without letting the yarn slip.

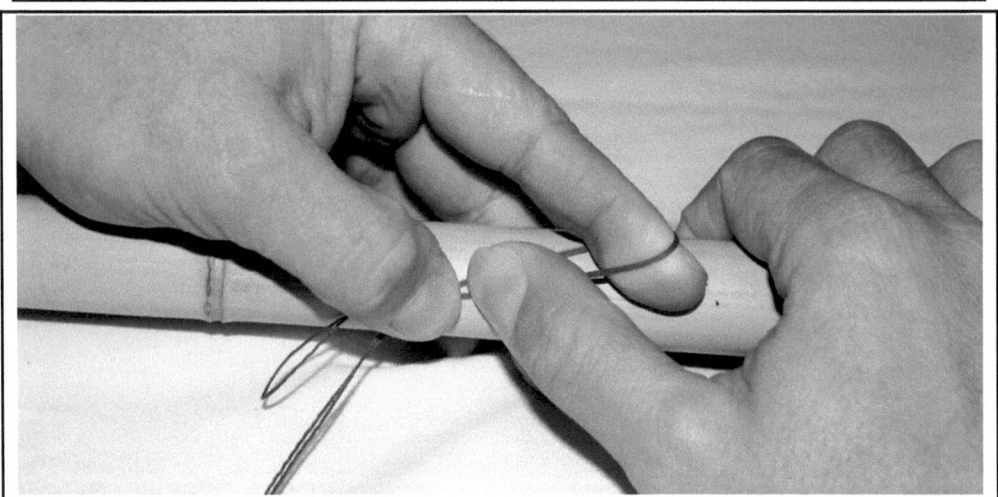

Figure 95: The same action as in the last illustration, shown from a different perspective. You can also notice that I used double yarn for this illustration. Essentially, it makes no difference, except that when using double yarn, you must ensure it does not twist around the tube while wrapping it.

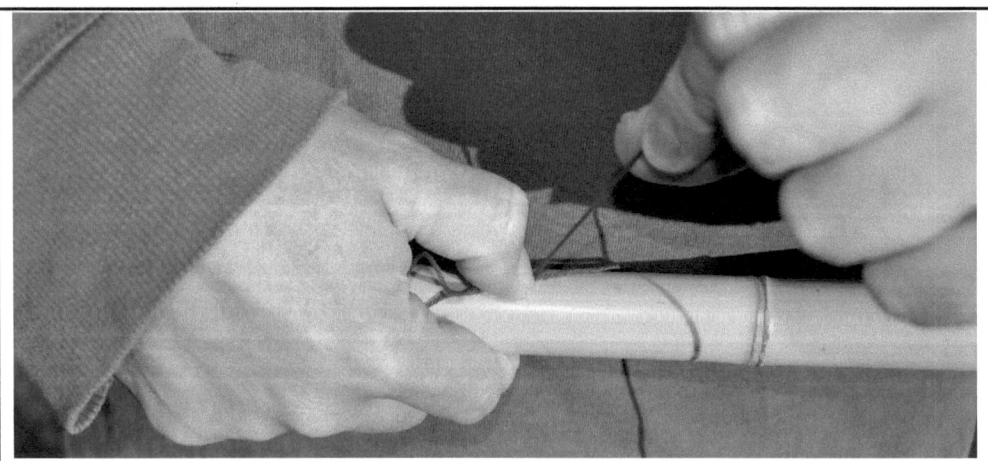

Figure 96: I hold the yarn firmly with my right thumb and begin to wrap the yarn around the tube with my left hand. However, this is done outward and toward the direction of the right hand.

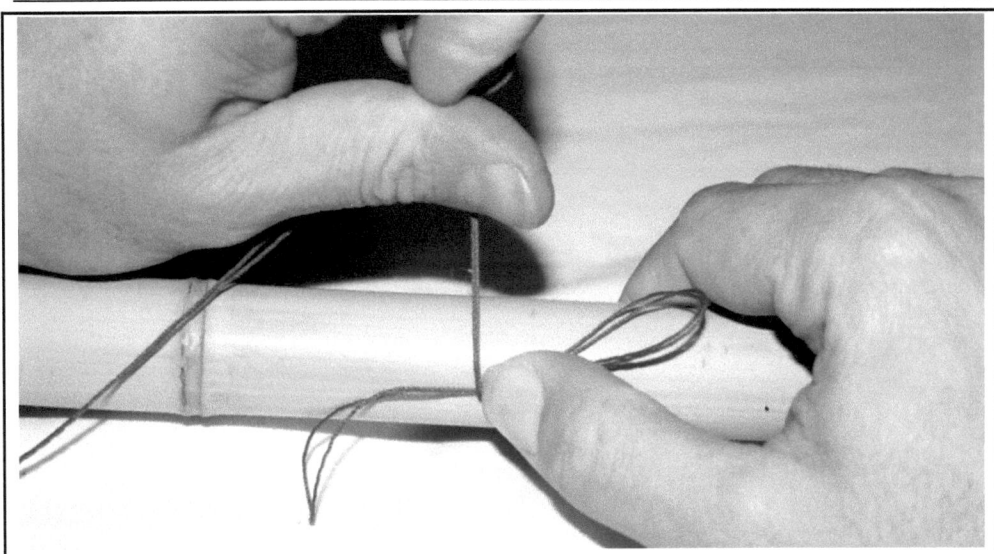

Figure 97: Once again, the same action as in the last image, just from a different perspective. You may have noticed by now that I used two bindings for the demonstration: one with single yarn from one perspective and the other with double yarn from another.

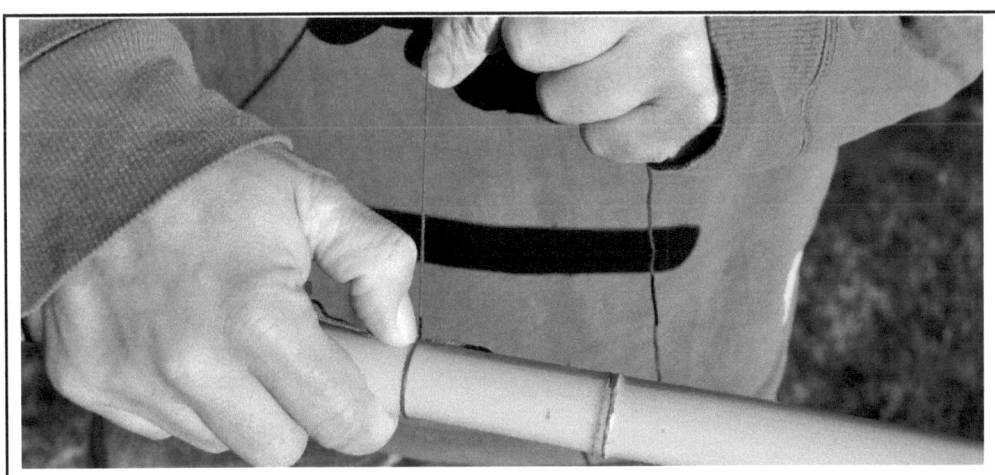

Figure 98: First wrapping completed. The yarn must be kept taut throughout the coming wrappings.

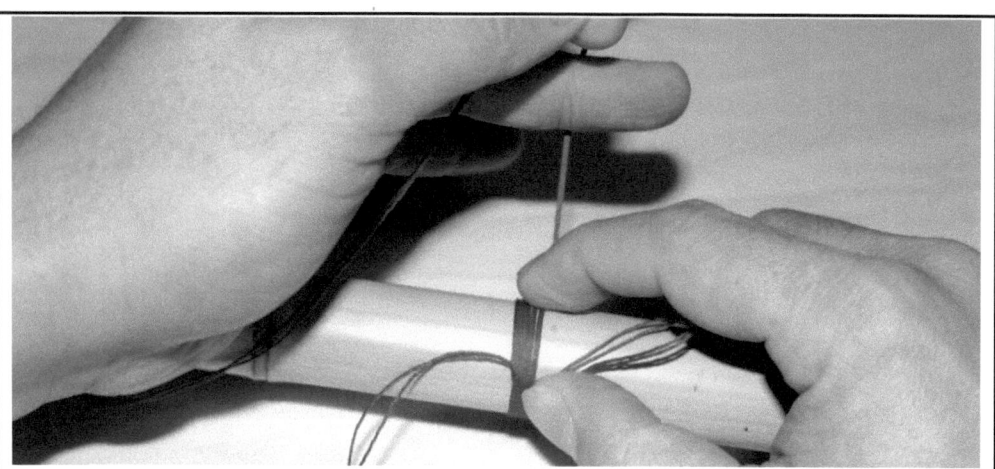

Figure 99: *While wrapping, the right index finger holds the yarn down so you can grasp the other end under the flute without becoming loose in the wrap. In this binding, I use two threads (double binding). On the right is the loop, and on the left is the end of the two threads, even though it appears like a loop in the image.*

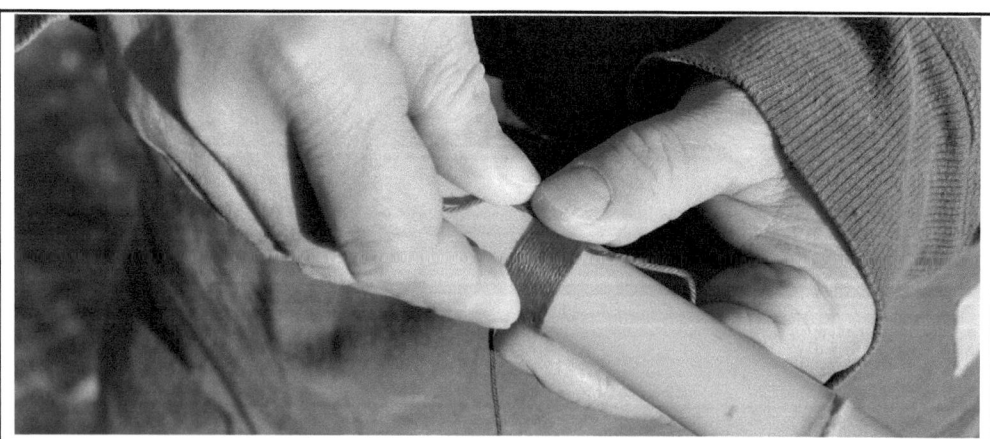

Figure 100: *When you have made enough tight wraps, it is time to prepare the knot. To do this, I hold the yarn at the "root" of the loop with my left thumb.*

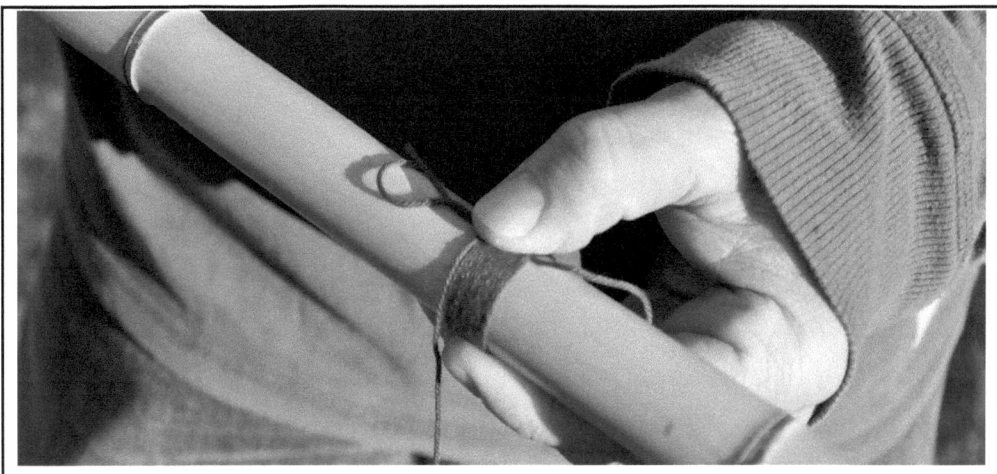

Figure 101: This leaves the left hand free to prepare the knot.

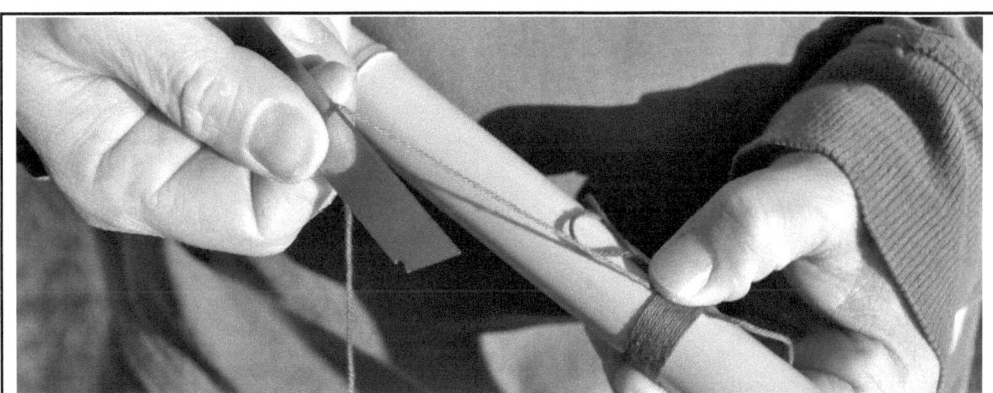

Figure 102: I now cut the other end to about 15 cm (5.90 in) with scissors or a cutter. Here I am holding a cutter in my right hand.

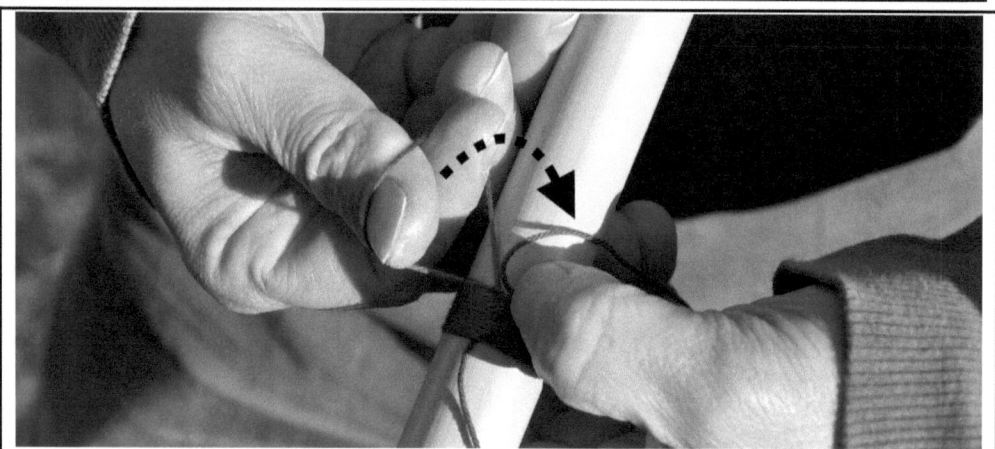

Figure 103: *I then use my right thumb and index finger to grasp the yarn, which is held under my left thumb, and pull it through the loop.* **Note:** *The loop is often twisted at the base, near the binding. This will prevent you from pulling the loop under the binding. You may need to twist the loop once or twice before proceeding with this step.*

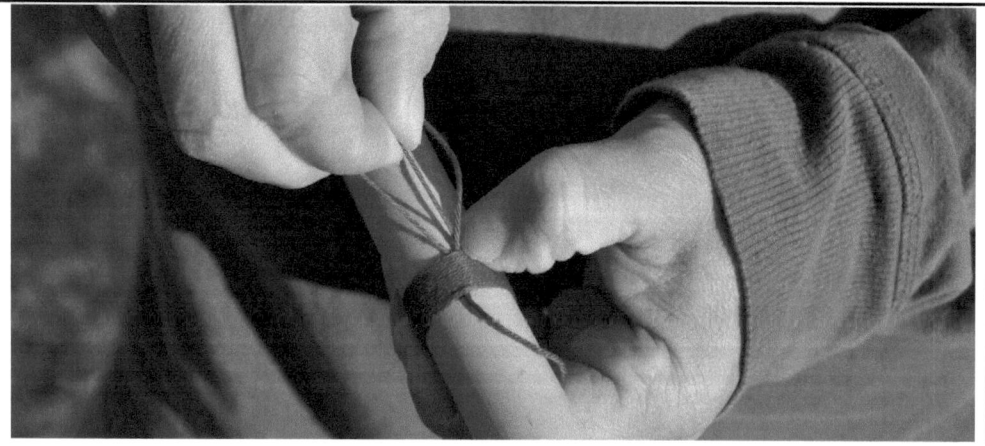

Figure 104: *Almost done. Make sure to continuously press down on the wrap and the end of the yarn in front of the loop with the thumb of your right hand. If it becomes loose, you might have to start all over again.*

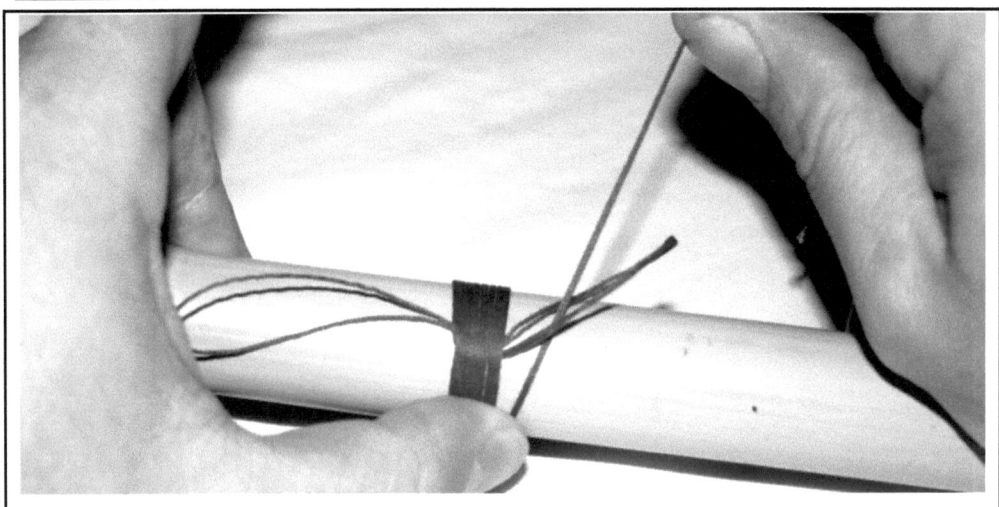

Figure 105: The same action as in the last image from a different perspective.

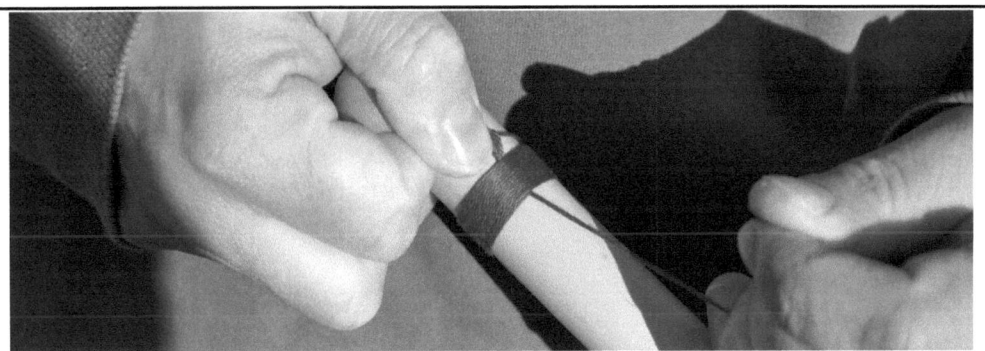

Figure 106: You must pull the first end to make the loop smaller until it pulls the freshly threaded end under the wrapping.

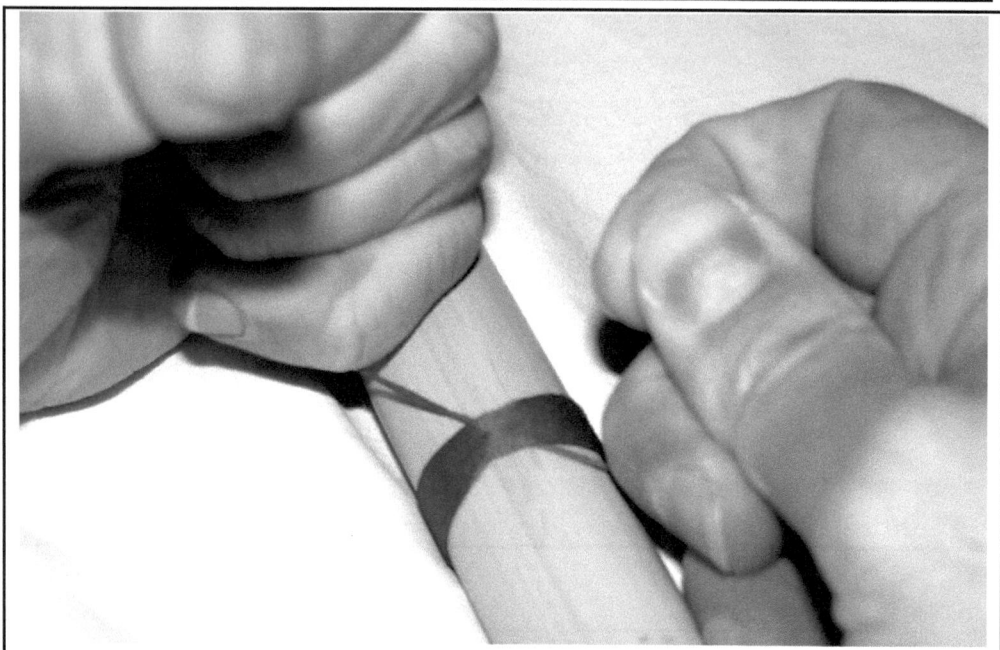

Figure 107: Just carefully adjust the knot under the center of the binding and pull it tight; not too much, or the yarn will break. You need to develop a feel for this. But with that, the binding is complete for now. **Note**: *Doing this often may cut the yarn into your skin. Therefore, I wear a soft leather glove on my left hand, which is not visible in the pictures. On my right hand, I have only the glove finger for my right ring finger cut so that all other fingers are free, as I need them unrestricted.*

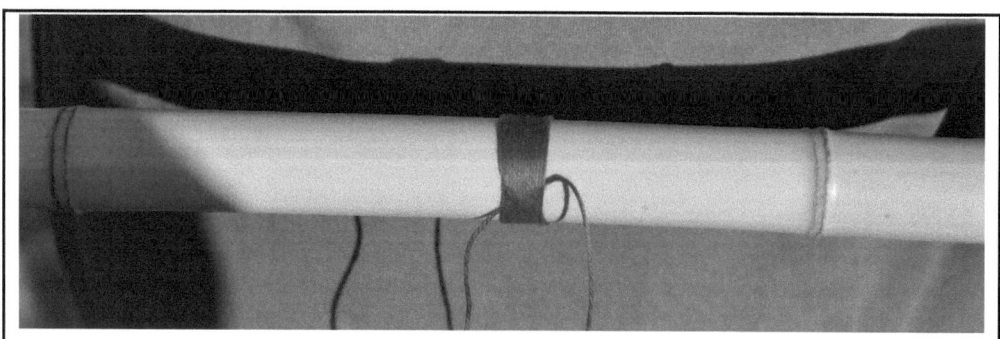

Figure 108: It might take a few attempts to master your binding, but you will succeed.

Figure 109: Now, all you need to do is trim the ends with a knife or cutter. I do not need to tell you that you could get hurt doing this, so wear gloves until you get the hang of it. Be careful; even after many years, I sometimes accidentally cut the yarn winding. It is better to double-check than to have to start all over again.

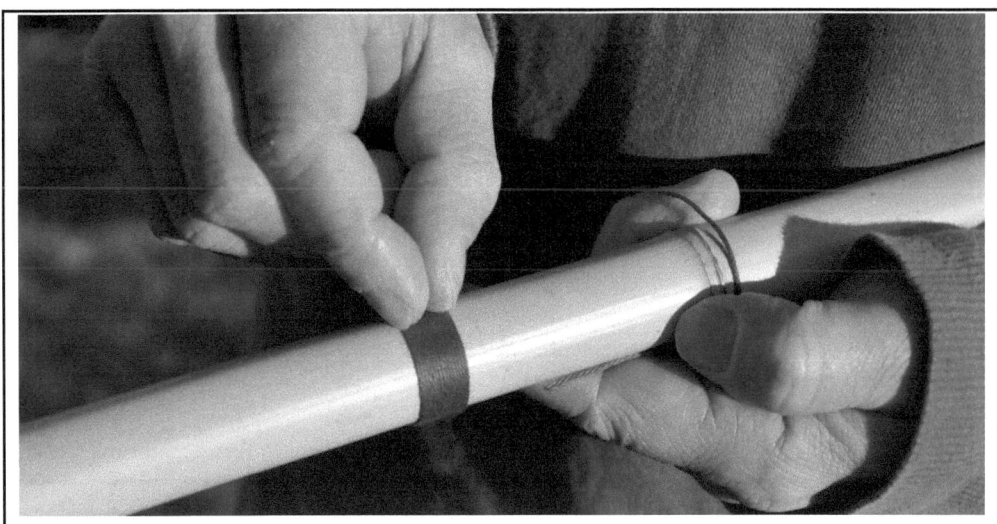

Figure 110: Finally, the winding can be gently compressed to eliminate any gaps or spaces.

Strengthening and Hardening the Bindings

Now that you have mastered your bindings, I offer you this tip. Natural yarn, whether cotton or linen, always has tiny fibers sticking up when lacquered with shellac. While this does not bother me personally, it can become an annoyance if you put the flute in a fabric bag or if some customers do not like it.

The hardening process I am showing you now makes the bindings tighter, stronger, and more stable, and the problem of loose fibers is also solved. The subsequent shellac coating will then give you a smooth surface.

How this works is explained in the following images, which show you every single step.

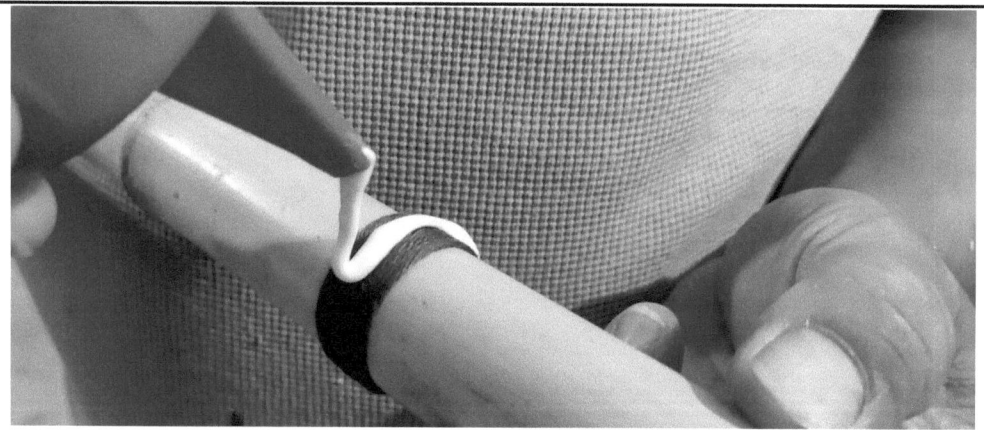

Figure 111: First, I apply a strip of wood glue to the binding using a tube. Caution: Some glue will constantly drip onto the floor! I have bought wood glue in a refillable tube and a bucket from the brand "Ponal." On one hand, it is solvent-free; on the other hand, it dries relatively quickly, which means you should work somewhat quickly.

However, this should not be a problem. It is not instant glue; you have about 10 minutes to work with it. If unsure, you can also buy wood glue that dries slowly.

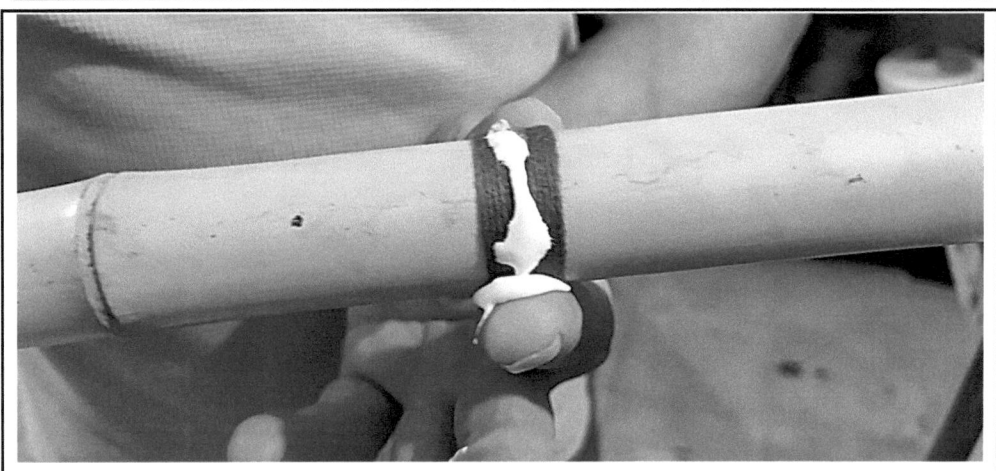

Figure 112: Here, you can see how I use my left hand with my index finger and thumb to smear the wood glue around the binding. I hold my index finger and thumb in position and use my right hand to rotate the flute around its longitudinal axis.

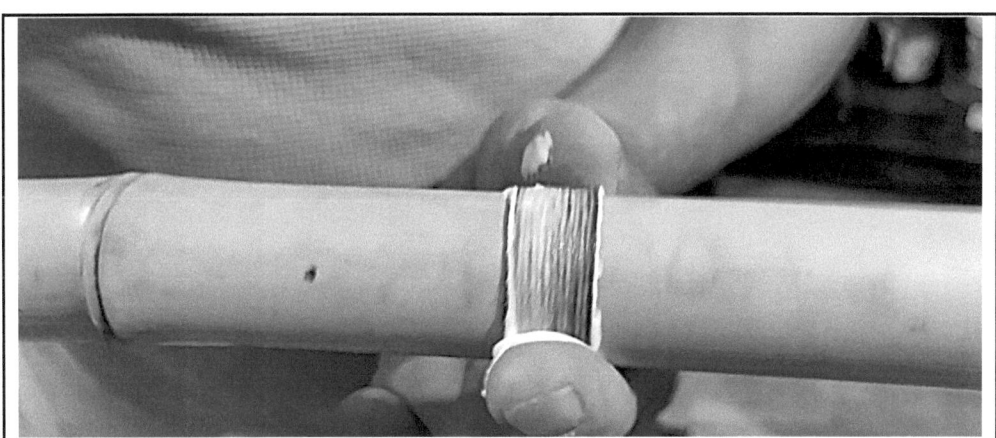

Figure 113: After rotating around the longitudinal axis once or twice, the wood glue is well distributed and has penetrated the yarn.

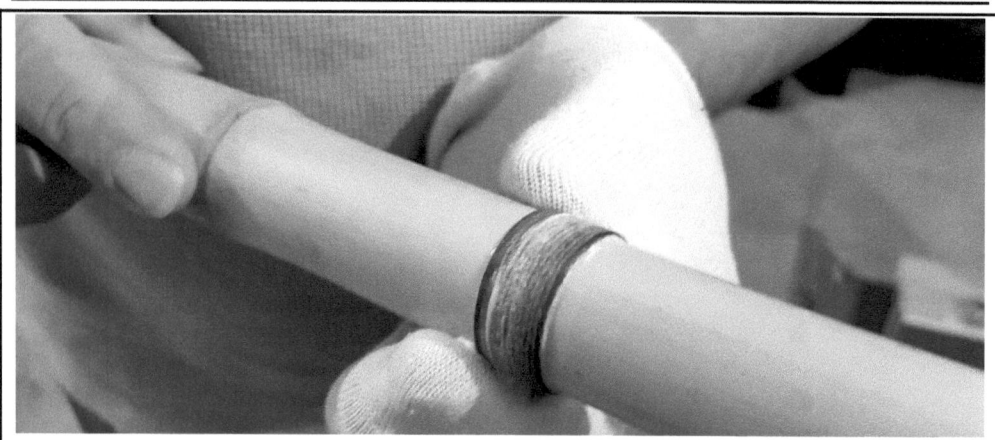

Figure 114: With a small cloth or one of the cheap socks, which I buy in bulk online for this purpose, I wipe off the excess wood glue on the left and right of the binding. I do this by rotating the flute while holding my left index finger and thumb on the side to be cleaned.

Figure 115: Finally, I run the glued binding through my left index finger and thumb once more to permanently flatten the protruding fibers against the binding. If necessary, I wipe the sides again if some glue is still there.

This process might seem cumbersome, but it only takes an extra 15 or 20 minutes. In return, your flutes will stand out with perfectly stable bindings. Since I started using this method for my bindings, I have never had a return from my customers. On the contrary, an international dealer who sells my shakuhachis to Japan has repeatedly mentioned that my bindings are particularly popular with his Japanese customers. So, I encourage you to master this method; it will make a difference in setting your flutes apart.

How many Bindings are Necessary?

I am often asked what the ideal number of bindings is. Should there be a binding between every finger hole, or are three or four bindings sufficient?

There is no definitive answer to this. If you work with bamboo often, you will develop a sense of it. Some tubes impress me so much that I feel confident without using any bindings, while I bind others as much as possible. It depends on each tube. Generally, I would recommend placing at least three bindings on a flute with six fingerholes, like the Kawala.

The Exterior Coating

You should also treat the outer surface of your flute. I will show you how to lacquer it with shellac. Of course, you can use a different lacquer, but in my experience, shellac is the best option. I recommend it for the reasons mentioned above.

The shellac for the flute's exterior should be slightly thinner than the one you used for the interior. The shellac polish from the " Clou " brand suits this purpose, or you can use the shellac you prepared yourself (see above).

You have probably already researched shellac treatment online. All the methods you have found are most probably meant for flat surfaces. In those cases, you first use some pumice powder in the mixture to close the wood pores, then sand the surface, and so forth.

For bamboo flutes, the challenge is shellac lacquering a round surface! If you are inexperienced, the shellac will drip off your flute's sides and form lumps. I have tried almost every method and eventually developed a rather unconventional method that, with very little practice, does not leave drips and is also the most cost-effective. Before starting your project, remember to protect your work surface. Instead of using only old newspapers, cut open a garbage bag, lay it on your work surface, and then spread the newspaper over it.

You will need an old bowl, a tile or an old plate, a new kitchen sponge, and scissors.

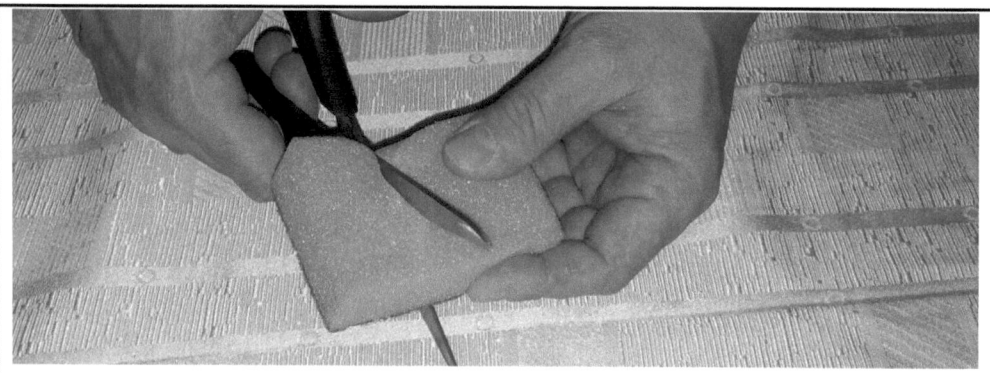

Figure 116: Using a high-quality kitchen sponge is essential to avoid leaving crumbs on lacquered surfaces. Be sure to cut the sponge into smaller pieces for better use. Avoid using an old sponge with grease and crumb remains.

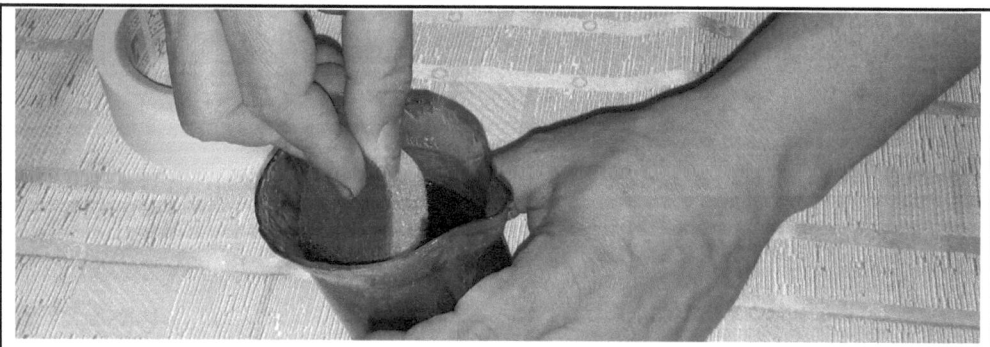

Figure 117: Now dip the tip of the cut kitchen sponge into the shellac. Try not to dip the rough side of the sponge into the shellac. This might not always be successful, but just keep it in mind.

Figure 118: Wipe off the excess shellac on the edge of the container by pressing down a little with your index finger on the top side. There is enough shellac on the sponge when it does not drip. It is better to have too little than too much! As you can see in the picture, getting shellac on your fingers is unavoidable. I do not use gloves because I can remove the shallack from my fingers with a bit of alcohol.

*Figure 119: This is how to apply shellac to the surface of your flute. Always stroke from the middle of the flute to the end. Then, rotate the flute slightly around its longitudinal axis and stroke again from the middle to the end. **Notice**: Shellac dries very quickly. You need to finish half of your flute within a minute or so. Be careful not to use too much shellac so it does not drip. It is better to use less and add another layer after fifteen minutes than to apply too much and get drips.*

I then place the flute on a tile. The tile is heavy enough not to slip and has a rough surface, so the flute itself cannot slip.

The lacquered side is down, and the side from which I held the flute during lacquering is up.

I lean the flute against the wall and wait about 15 minutes. By then, the shellac is already dry enough for me to work on the other half of the flute.

I repeat this process so that the flute is fully lacquered three times. Finally, the flute needs to rest.

Anyhow, if I am in a good mood and the customer requests it, I repeat this lacquering process twice on two consecutive days,

Please remember, it takes 10-14 days for the shellac to harden fully, though you can play the flute already after a couple of hours.

Congratulations! You have mastered your Kawala. You really may be proud of yourself.

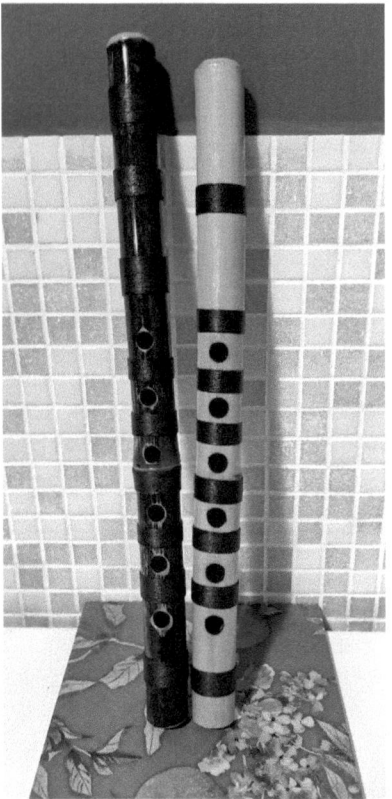

Figure 120: Two Kawala flutes lacquered and drying.

The following section will give tips on special bindings and tunings for Kawalas.

Special Tunings for Kawalas

We have seen that the Kawala can be easily tuned to a major scale. You simply need to divide the length of the flute by 12 and drill holes at positions 2, 3, 4, 5, 6, and 7 from the bottom, tuning them accordingly. The whole-step and half-step structure between the notes is as follows:

Whole-Whole-Half-Whole-Whole-Whole-Half

or the formula: **0-2-2-1-2-2-2-1**

How do we then Construct a Kawala on a Minor Scale?

Using the harmonic minor scale example, I will explain the special tunings on the Kawala, and you can apply this calculation method to any other tuning. The harmonic minor scale has a slightly different whole-step and half-step structure:

Whole – Half – Whole – Whole – Half – Whole and a half – Half

or the formula: **0-2-1-2-2-1-3-1**

Let us apply this to our working table as we learned above, using the example of the C minor scale:

C	C#	D	D#	E	F	F#	G	G#	A	A#	H
0		2	1		2		2	1			3
C	C#	D	D#	E	F	F#	G	G#	A	A#	H
1											

Thus, the notes of the C harmonic minor scale would be:

C-D-Eb-F-G-Ab-B-C

In contrast, the major scale has the following notes:

C-D-E-F-G-A-B-C

If we compare the major and harmonic minor scales in two tables side by side, the differences become more explicit (I am omitting the high C here):

Major	C	C#	D	D#	E	F	F#	G	G#	A	A#	B
	1		2		2	1		2		2		2

Harm. Minor	C	C#	D	D#	E	F	F#	G	G#	A	A#	B
	0		2	1		2		2	1			3

In short, the holes for E and A in the major scale must be shifted lower to provide D♯ (Eb) and G♯ (Ab) in the harmonic minor scale. Therefore, they must each be drilled a half step lower. The following three images illustrate how to derive the positions of the minor scale from a calculation for a major Kawala:

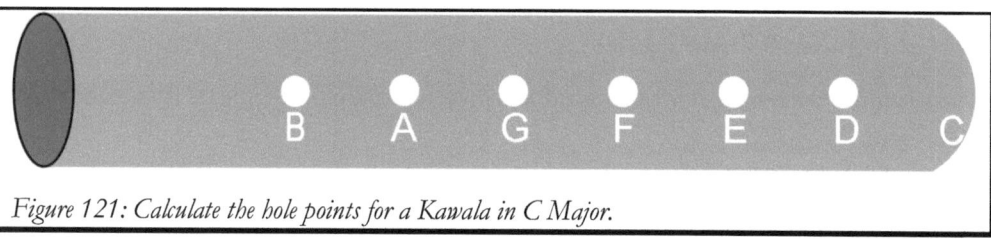

Figure 121: Calculate the hole points for a Kawala in C Major.

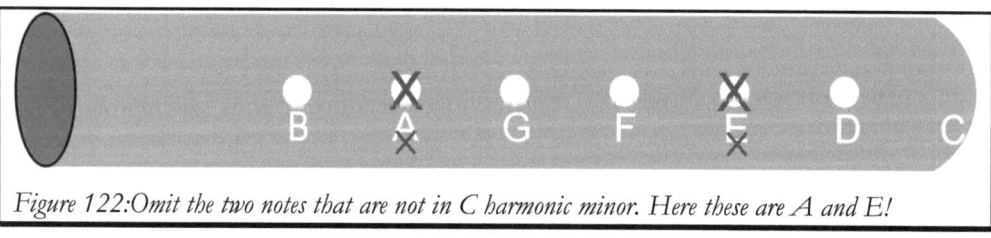

Figure 122: Omit the two notes that are not in C harmonic minor. Here these are A and E!

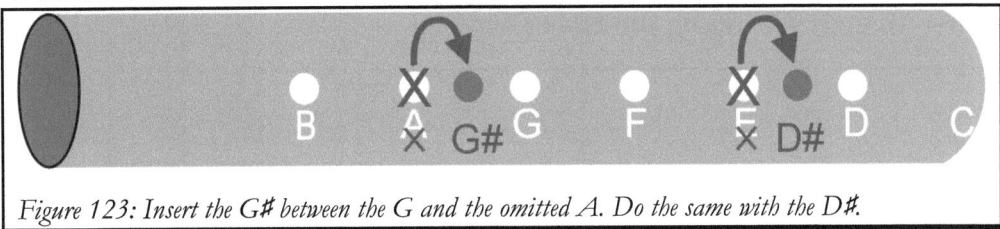

Figure 123: Insert the G♯ between the G and the omitted A. Do the same with the D♯.

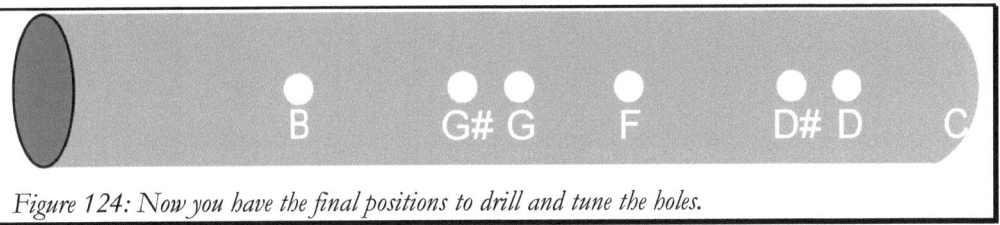

Figure 124: Now you have the final positions to drill and tune the holes.

Oversized Kawalas

There is a current preference for large bamboo flutes. Bamboo flutes have an exotic, meditative quality! With large flutes, you can achieve deep, sonorous tones but cannot play fast pieces as easily.

The main challenge with large flutes is that the position of the holes and the distance between them must always be proportional to the size of the flute. At a certain point, the flute becomes so large that you can only cover the holes with your hands and feet.

Kawalas can still be played up to 60 cm in length, but it gradually becomes more difficult as the flute becomes longer because the distance between the holes becomes larger. There are three methods to address this:

1. **First Method:** Reduce the distance between the holes by changing the hole diameter.
2. **Second Method:** Adjust the hole positions along the longitudinal axis.
3. **Third Method:** Combine methods (1) and (2).

First Method: Changing the Hole Diameter

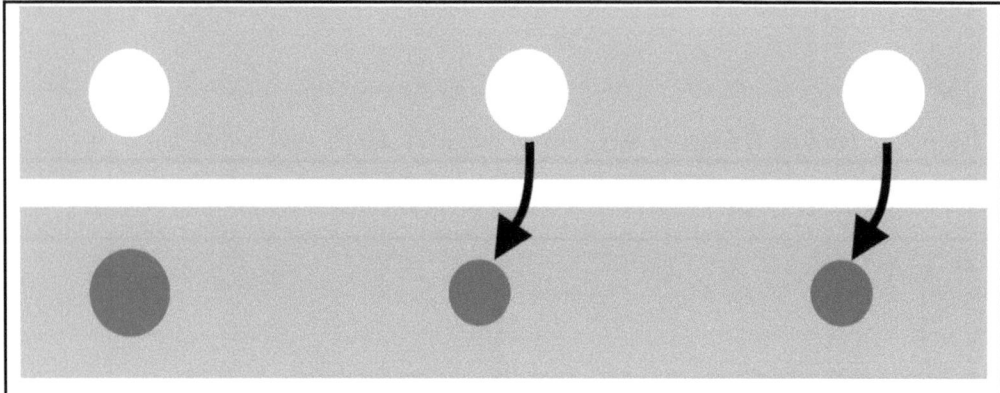

Figure 125: At the top is a flute with precisely calculated hole positions (white holes). At the bottom is a flute with adjusted hole positions (gray holes).

Take a look at this image. I have shown two flute sections with three holes each. The top flute has uniformly sized holes in the mathematically correct position.

When reading about tuning, you have learned two rules:

1. The smaller the hole, the lower the pitch!
2. The higher the hole is placed toward the blowing edge, the higher the pitch!

This means you can move a hole slightly upward by reducing the planned hole diameter. For example, if you reduce the hole diameter by 1 mm (approximately 10-15 cents lower), you can also place the hole about 2 mm higher, which would correct it by 10-15 cents higher. This also means that you could position a hole nearer to the bottom of the flute and make the diameter bigger.

Whatever way you choose, you definitely need to buy two pipes with the same diameter and test this feature yourself. These nuances are what distinguish good bamboo flute makers. You must gain your own experience in this area.

Second Method: Adjusting Hole Positions Along the Longitudinal Axis

As you read these lines, I ask you to look at the back of your left hand briefly. Spread your index, middle, and ring fingers as far apart as possible.

Now, draw an imaginary line connecting all your fingernails.

What will this line look like?

It will be a curve, with the middle finger almost forming the radius!

If your flute were curved, you would have the perfect fingers to play it.

Covering the holes of a slightly larger flute with just your fingertips is almost impossible!

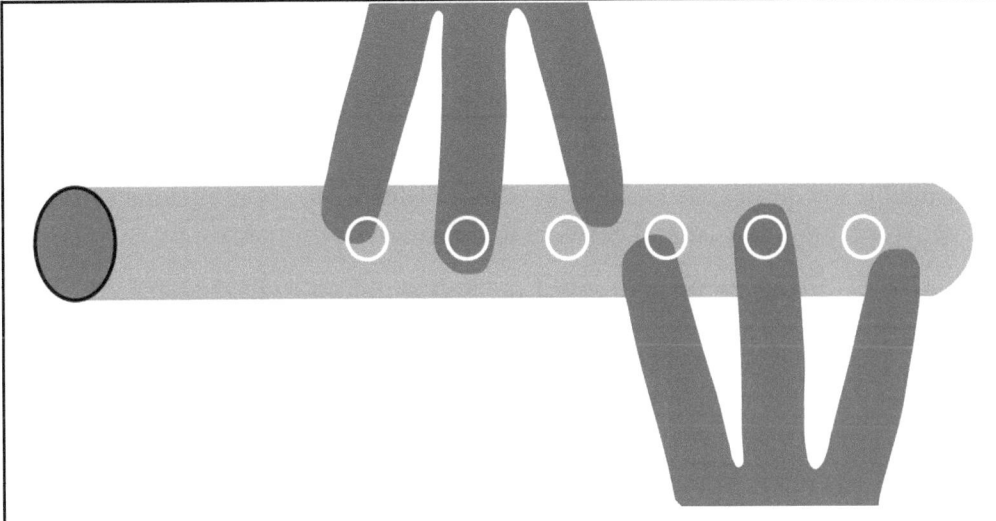

Figure 126: **Top:** *The left hand's index, middle, and ring fingers. Since our fingers are of different lengths, only one hole can be covered easily.*

Bottom: *Index, middle, and ring fingers of the right hand. The same problem occurs with the left hand.*

One solution would be to cover the holes with your entire fingers:

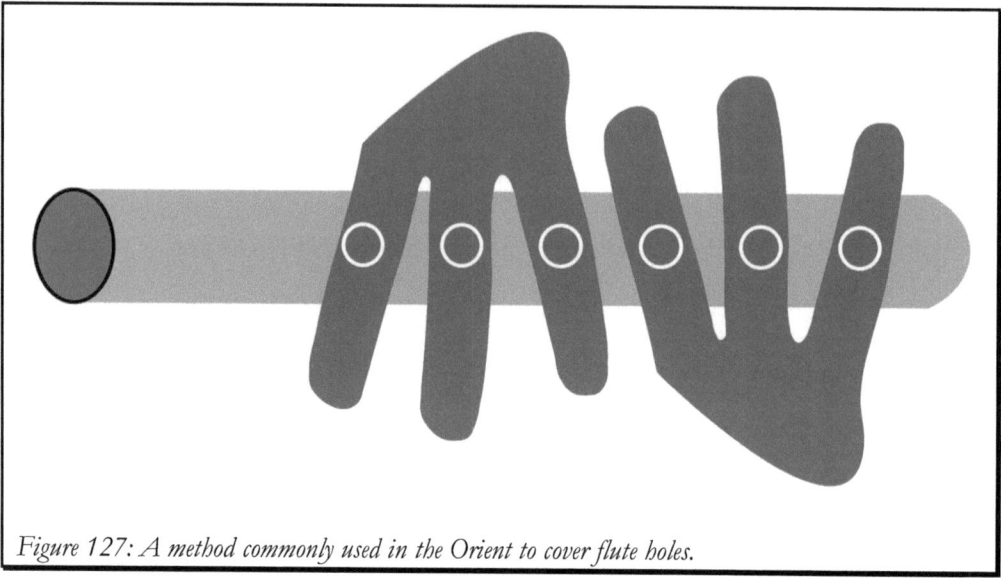

Figure 127: A method commonly used in the Orient to cover flute holes.

Although this method makes sliding from one note to the next very easy, it is unsuitable for quick note changes. It is more suitable for calm melodies. In any case, you cannot play large flutes very well this way!

Therefore, the suggestion is to adjust the hole positions to fit the hand:

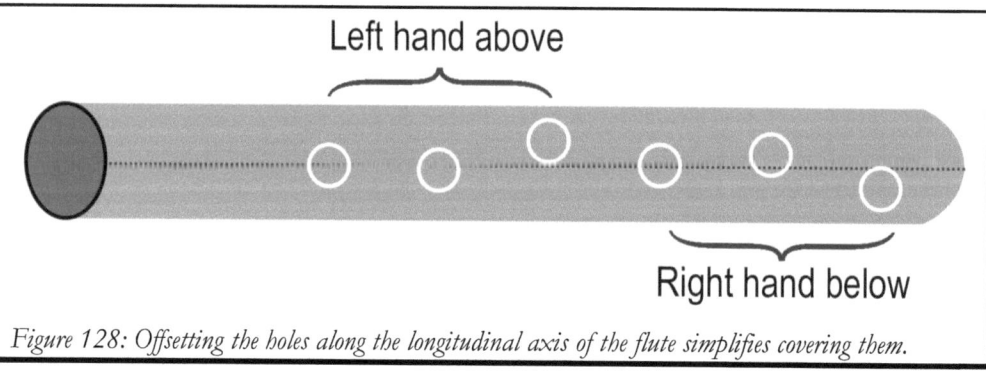

Figure 128: Offsetting the holes along the longitudinal axis of the flute simplifies covering them.

Suddenly, it is much easier to cover the holes in the flute with your fingertips.

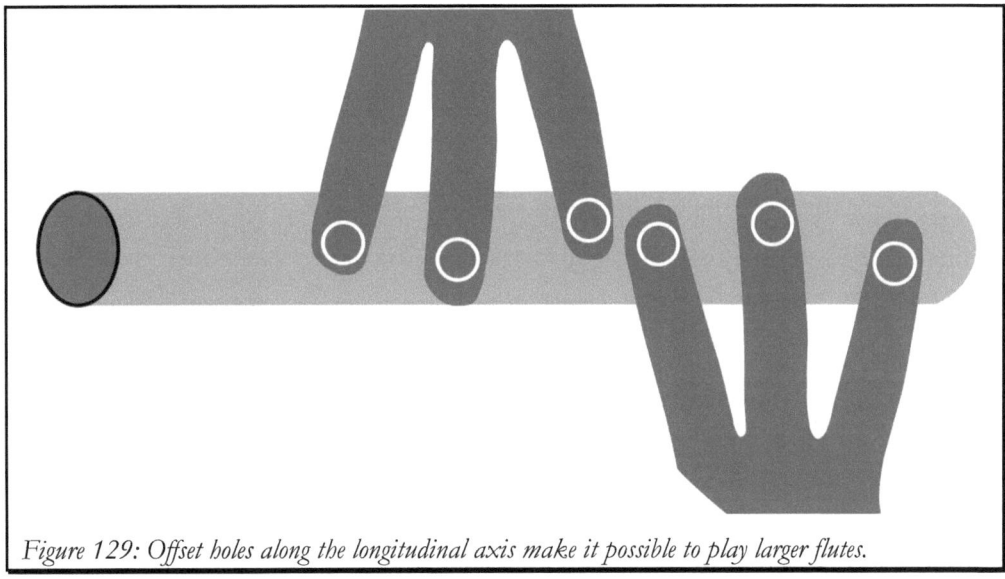

Figure 129: Offset holes along the longitudinal axis make it possible to play larger flutes.

Third Method: Combine Methods (1) and (2).

Of course, you can combine both methods, adjusting the holes along the longitudinal axis while reducing the distance between them by changing their diameter. I use this method, especially for people with one or more missing fingertips.

Before we leave the Kawala

In about 100 pages, I offered you almost everything I have learned and experienced over the years about Kawalas. If you have understood and practiced it, welcome to the world of the oldest wind instrument, the Kawala. Knowledge of its construction and tuning is foundational for building almost any rim-blown flute. In this book, we will also build four more flutes: two Saluang flutes from Indonesia, the Pueblo Broken Cave Flute (BCF), and the Ney. With the BCF, I will guide you through replicating archaic flutes. But let us start with the simpler Saluang flutes.

Build the Saluang Flutes

Saluang flutes are the Indonesian version of the Kawala, played mainly by the Minangkabau people. They merely differ in the amount of holes. As you have learned in the last Chapter, "Special Tunings for Kawalas," how to calculate different hole positions for different tunings, building the Salunag Flutes becomes pretty easy. Salunag Flutes (in plural) because there are several tunings the Minangkabau people use. We shall discuss the Salunag Darek and the Saluang Sirompak here.

The Saluang Darek

If you know how to calculate the hole positions of a Kawala, you already have all you need for the Saluang Darek because it uses only the first five notes of a Major scale. So if you use a C-Major scale for our Saluang Darek, you need the C, D, E, F, and G. And if you want a Saluang Darek on E, you need the E, F#, G#, A, and B.

It is really as simple as that. In other words, you only need the first four holes from the bottom up of a Kawala to build a Salunag Darek.

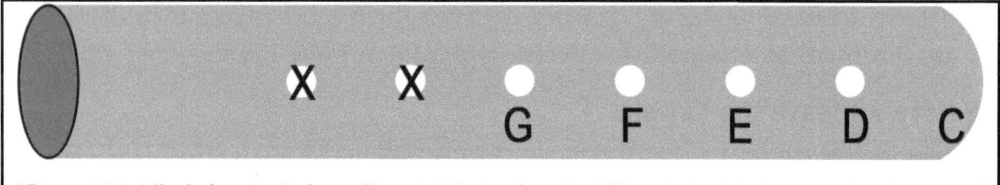

Figure 130: The holes of a Saluang Darek. Notice that the fifth and sixth holes are omitted compared to the Kawala.

The Saluang Sirompak

The Saluang Sirompak may seem tricky to build, but it is easy. The traditional Salunag Sirompak plays the following notes:

$$F - A - C - D - E$$

If you think of it, it is nothing but an F-Major:

$$F - G - A - Bb - C - D - E$$

The Saluang Sirompak simply omits the G and Bb

F – ( ) – A – ( ) – C – D – E

This means that all you need to do is imagine the hole positions of a Kawala in F and forget about the holes Nr. 1 and 3 from the bottom up.

As the fundamental Note is an "F," you need a long reed between 70 and 75 cm, depending on the inner diameter of your flute.

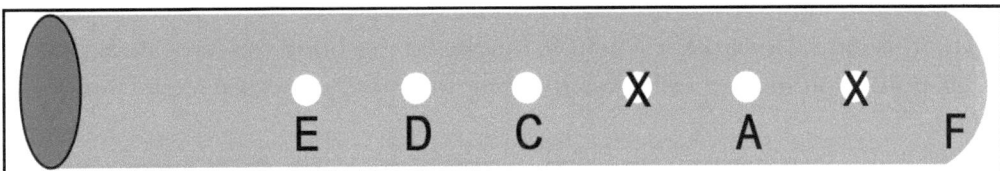

Figure 131: The Saluang Sirompak. Compared to the Kawala, the first and second holes are just omitted. It cannot get easier than that.

However, do not limit yourself to the standard F tuning in a Saluang or any other flute.

If you want to pursue making rim-blown flutes as a profession, take into account the varied needs of your potential customers.

People with smaller hands may find instruments tuned to C, D, or E, or even higher, more comfortable and playable.

There are endless possibilities for instrument modification. For example, converting the E hole into a thumb hole could introduce new playing techniques.

Adapting the instrument to suit individual players is not disrespectful to its cultural heritage but rather a powerful tool for making the music of other cultures more accessible to a broader audience. In fact, this principle forms the basis of the entire philosophy of this book.

Build the Puebloan (Anasazi) Flute

I stumbled online on colleagues building and selling Anasazi Flutes over a decade ago. According to the Indian Pueblo Cultural Center[1], the term Anasazi, however, means "ancient enemy," and the Pueblo people understandably do not like to be preferred too with such a term. Hence, I will be using the term Puebloan Flute here. However, I humbly ask for forgiveness, having included the term Anasazi in the book's title. It was necessary because the flute has widely become known with this term. However, if you have purchased this book and have studied it to this point, you may as well consider using the more respectful term "Puebloan Flute."

We will simply use the term "Broken Cave Flute" (BCF) when referring to the Puebloan Flutes discovered in the Prayer Rock district of NorthEastern Arizona in 1931 by Earl H. Morris, leading an exhibition of the Carnegie Institution of Washington. Four flutes were found, which are exceptionally well preserved and date back to 620-670 AD. Each has six finger holes. I strongly recommend reading the paper by Bakkegard and Morris (1961) on these flutes.[2] At least visit the Arizona State Museum website and watch what they look like.[3]

Modern flute builders in the US have added Shakuhachi-style blowing Edges to the Puebloan flutes, not necessarily because it makes them better, but I guess because playing a Shakuhachi is by far easier than a rim-blown flute like a Kawala, Saluang, BCF or Ney. The spread of the Kawala genre flutes in the world in prehistoric ages may have sparked creating blowing edges and developed into Shakuhahis. However, I will deal with Shakuhachis in my next book.

Bakkegard and Morris (1961) published the lengths and hole positions of the four Broken Cave Flutes (BCF 1-4) in their paper.

---

[1] https://indianpueblo.org/
[2] Bakkegard, B. M., & Morris, E. A. (1961). Seventh Century Flutes from Arizona. Ethnomusicology, 5(3), 184–186. https://doi.org/10.2307/924518
[3]   https://www.statemuseum.arizona.edu/online-exhibit/ancestral-pueblo-flutes-broken-flute-cave

Next, I will take you on a tour of how I calculate the hole positions of archaic flutes using the example of the BCF.

At first, I copied the lengths of BCF 1-4 into Excel and calculated the Length/12 (LV) variable, which we used to build our Kawala:

	Length	LV
BCV-1	73.5	6.13
BCV-2	72.3	6.03
BCV-3	68.5	5.71
BCV-3	68.5	5.71

BCF-Calculation-Table 1: Broken Cave Flutes (Lengths and LV's)

In the next step, I added the six hole Positions (Counted from the Bottom to the Blowing edge). Bakkegard and Morris (1961) used the metric system to indicate the positions of the holes:

	H1	H2	H3	H4	H5	H6
BCV-1	11.70 cm	15.90 cm	20.00 cm	29.00 cm	33.20 cm	37.00 cm
BCV-2	11.00 cm	14.90 cm	19.20 cm	28.40 cm	32.50 cm	36.50 cm
BCV-3	10.60 cm	14.40 cm	19.40 cm	26.30 cm	32.20 cm	36.1 cm
BCV-4	12.00 cm	16.40 cm	20.10 cm	30.10 cm	34.10 cm	36.20 cm

BCF-Calculation-Table 2: Hole Positions in cm of the BCFs

Notice the space between H3 and H4 because the holes are bundled in two groups with almost identical distances. Three holes below and three above.

In the third step, I calculated the distances using the LV-Variable:

	H1	H2	H3	H4	H5	H6
BCV-1	1.9 LV	2.6 LV	3.3 LV	4.7 LV	5.4 LV	6 LV
BCV-2	1.8 LV	2.5 LV	3.2 LV	4.7 LV	5.4 LV	6.1 LV
BCV-3	1.9 LV	2.5 LV	3.4 LV	4.6 LV	5.6 LV	6.3 LV
BCV-4	2.1 LV	2.9 LV	3.5 LV	5.3 LV	6 LV	6.3 LV

BCF-Calculation-Table 3: Hole Positions of the BCV using the LV-Variable

Finally, I calculated the LV-Variable Average (LV-AVG) of all four flutes:

	H1	H2	H3	H4	H5	H6
LV-AVG	1.93 LV	2.63 LV	3.35 LV	4.83 LV	5.60 LV	6.18 LV

BCF-Calculation-Table 4: LV- Average Hole Positions

Let us shortly remember the Kawala Positions:

	H1	H2	H3	H4	H5	H6
Kawala	2 LV	3 LV	4 LV	5 LV	6 LV	7 LV

BCF-Calculation-Table 5: Kawala LV Hole Positions

The reference frequency for 440 or 432 Hz tuning instruments did not exist in seventh-century North America. We can try to unify the positions to meet modern tunings with the knowledge we have gained.

In the first attempt, we could round the LV-AVG for the BCF to a reasonable factor for Western musicians (LV-West). Compare the L-AVG with the L-West here:

	H1	H2	H3	H4	H5	H6
LV-AVG	1.93 LV	2.63 LV	3.35 LV	4.83 LV	5.60 LV	6.18 LV
LV-West	2 LV	2.5 LV	3.5 LV	5 LV	5.5 LV	6 LV

BCF-Calculation-Table 6: Rounded LV Hole Positions for the BCF

Using this calculation formula, you can easily rebuild a Puebloan BCF, which can be played along with Western Harmonies.

However, you will notice a problem in the H3 hole of the BCF. To understand this, let us recall the abovementioned C-Major scale calculation. The following table compares three rows: The chromatic Scale (CS), the C-Major Scale (C+), and the Kawala LV-Faktor calculation (K-LV).

Chr.	C	C#	D	D#	E	F	F#	G	G#	A	A#	B
C+	C		D		E	F		G		A		B
KLF	0 LV		2 LV		3 LV	4 LV		5 LV		6 LV		7 LV

BCF-Calculation-Table 7: Recalling the Kawala Hole Calculation.

Using the L-West, we calculated in the BCF-Calculation-Table 6 (previous page) that we should have our third hole at **3.5 L**. However, on a major scale, the distance between the third note (second hole) and the fourth note (third hole) is only half a note. This means we would have a note between E and F in the C-Major, which cannot be played on a chromatic scale because the distance between E and F is only half a note.

You will have to make a compromise and either lower the third hole to **3 L** or raise it to **4 L**.

You would then have one of the following situations: BCF-Lowered (BCF-L) or BCF Raised (BCF-R)

Chr.	C	C#	D	D#	E	F	F#	G	G#	A
BCF-L	0 LV		2 LV	2.5 LV	3 LV			5 LV	5.5 LV	6 LV
BCF-R	0 LV		2 LV	2.5 LV		4 LV		5 LV		6 LV

BCF-Calculation-Table 8: Lowered and Raised BCF Solutions for Western Music.

Nevertheless, the Puebloan BCF looks strikingly similar to Ney flutes, which we will deal with in the following chapter. Hence, after going through building the Ney, I strongly encourage you to return to this Chapter and consider building the BCFs with quartertones as the Ney.

If you recall the quarter tones we mentioned in the introduction, these notes falling between the half-steps can be easily drilled on flutes by drilling the holes halfway between the chromatic notes.

Hence, I am adding a third tuning option (BCF-O), closest to the LV-AVG calculated in the BCF-Calculation-Table 6 above. It includes the quarter notes for the BCF.

Here, the third Option (BCF-O) is compared to the LV-AVG.

	H1	H2	H3	H4	H5	H6
Notes	D	D#	E$\ddagger$	G$\flat$	G#	A
LV-AVG	1.93 LV	2.63 LV	3.35 LV	4.83 LV	5.6 LV	6.18 LV
BCF-O	2LV	2.5 LV	3.5 LV	4.75 LV	5.5 LV	6 LV

BCF-Calculation-Table 9: Third Tuning Option with Quarter Tones (P3O)

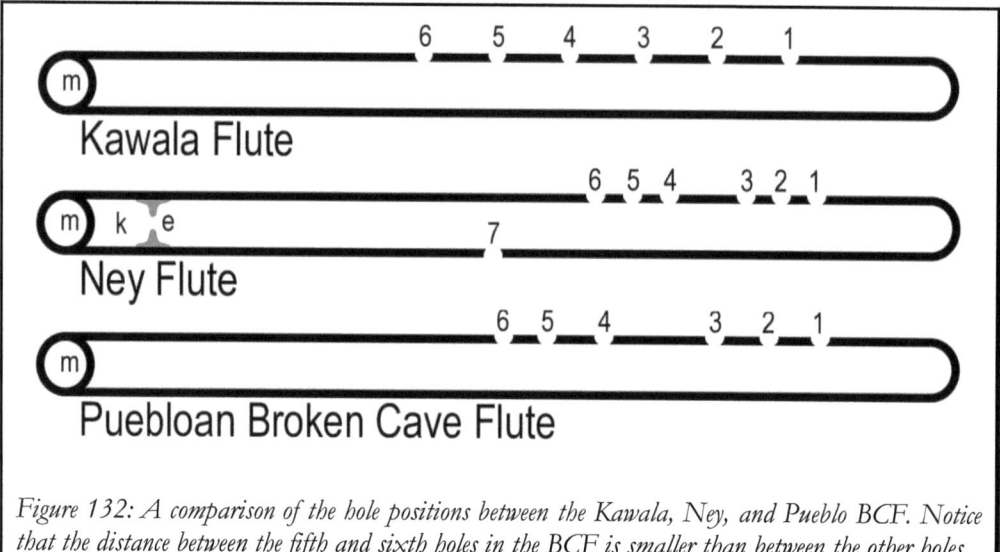

Figure 132: A comparison of the hole positions between the Kawala, Ney, and Pueblo BCF. Notice that the distance between the fifth and sixth holes in the BCF is smaller than between the other holes.

Finally, it rests in your decision which tuning you choose. Unlike the Salunag, Kawala, and Ney, the musical tradition of playing the BCF has not been handed over for generations, and we will never be 100% sure of the tuning.

Let me give you another small aid to build the BCF. Once you have decided on a hole-calculation system, I highly suggest that you calculate the percentages. Like that, you can calculate the hole positions even faster. For my calculated LV-AVG, this would be the following:

	H1	H2	H3		H4	H5	H6
Notes	D	D#	E♯		G♭	G#	A
LV-AVG	1.93 LV	2.63 LV	3.35 LV		4.83 LV	5,6 LV	6,18 LV
% - AVG	16,32%	22,20%	28,35%		40,99%	47,55%	52,51%

Remember that calculations are not always perfect because each bamboo reed is individual, and indeed, the diameter and thickness of your bamboo play a significant role.

When I approach building a new flute with the reeds I have, which are pretty similar in diameter and thickness, I usually have two or three failed attempts before I have my blank for further flutes. So, keep the custom of drilling the holes smaller than their target diameter and take them from the lowest to the upper hole step by step.

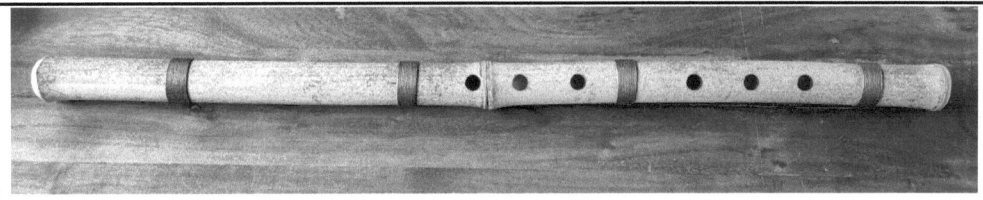

Figure 133: Puebloan Broken Cave Flute on C. I have built this flute just now between writing these sentences, as I have not done this for years, according to the percentages shown in the last table above, without taking a careful tuning approach. As expected, the fifth and sixth holes failed. Had I not had my standard blanc for this flute, I would have given it a second or possible third attempt.

As you start adapting, fitting, and tuning, you will begin to improve your flute-building skills.

Here is a composite image of a flute, showing the front side on top and the bottom side on the bottom:

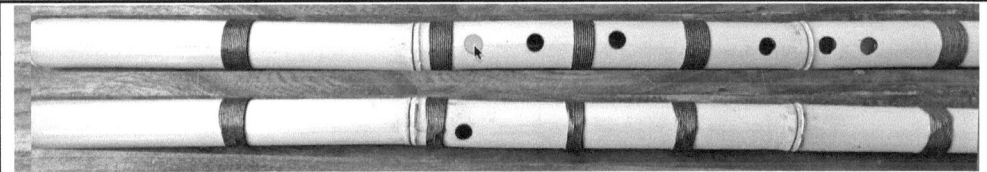

Figure 134: Please note that the sixth hole is only marked in the upper section, not drilled. To simplify fingering, I converted this hole into a thumb hole (see the lower section), which does not change the tuning. Additionally, I shifted the fourth hole slightly for easier reach with my ring finger.

If you live in the US or have extensively searched online to buy a Puebloan BCF, you may have noticed that the blowing edge has been altered to resemble a Shakuhachi blowing edge.

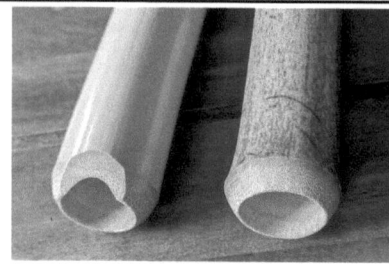

This is not a hindrance; on the contrary, it allows for nuanced sound variations. In my opinion, it is essential that, unlike with the Shakuhachi, the flute is sanded all around like the Kawala so that it can be played straight or on the edge, producing more tonal colors.

Figure 135: Original Form on the right and modern blowing edge added on the left.

On the right side, I have photographed two flutes in progress. On the left is a Shakuhachi, and on the right is the Pueblo BCF.

Hopefully, you can see the difference.

While the Shakuhachi has a notch and remains as thick-walled as possible, except for a slight curve on the opposite side of the notch to press better against the chin, you can see how the

Figure 136: Shakuhachi on the left versus enhanced modern BCF on the right.

Pueblo BCF has a sharp edge ground all around, allowing it to be played in any position, as I will demonstrate in the following page.

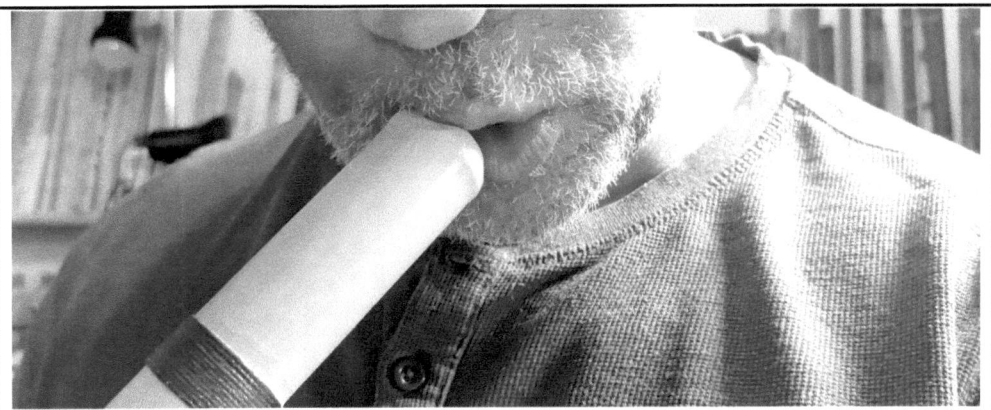

Figure 137: I am playing the Pueblo BCF as it was originally thought to be played in the seventh century A.D. However, looking closely, you can see a bevel on the upper end of the flute's mouthpiece. This is a blowing notch inspired by the Shakuhachi, although it is not as deep as on a Shakuhachi; otherwise, the air would escape.

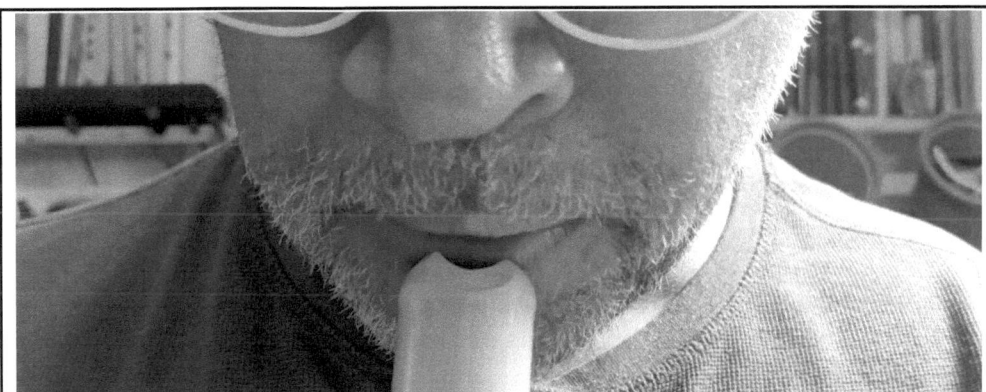

Figure 138: Here, you can see that I am playing the same flute as the previous image, like a Shakuhachi. However, you must be more careful since the notch is smaller than a Shakuhachi. It might take some time, but soon, you will know how to blow it correctly.

This is the moment where I think you should watch my online video about rim-blown flutes, where I compare different blowing techniques. The video is uploaded to YouTube and titled "Rim Blown or Side Blown Technique for Ney-Ney, Kawala, Pueblo (Anasazi), and Other Flutes."

If you have your smartphone in hand, you can watch the video directly via the QR code on the right.

Figure 139: YouTube Film about rim blown flutes

While I hope the video, which has been online for several years, and the following one will not be deleted, I cannot guarantee they will remain on YouTube forever.

To hear the potential of the Pueblo BCFs, I invite you to watch a video of mine on YouTube that is now over ten years old, titled "Pueblo (Anasazi) Flute & Ewi 4000." In this video, I play the BCF using both methods alternately, along with an Akai EWI. However, I would also like to apologize for not knowing at the time what the word "Anasazi" meant and that the Pueblo people do not like this term.

After watching the YouTube videos, it is time to learn how to add the blowing edge notch to the Puebloan BCF. For this purpose, my son took photos of me going through each step.

Figure 140: Pueblo Flute with Ewi from Akai.

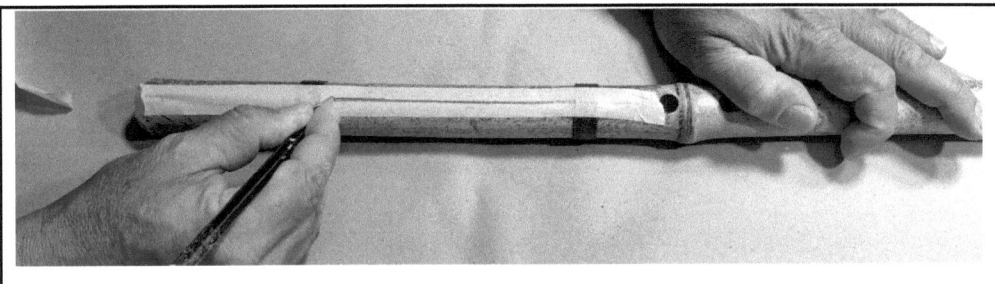

Figure 141: I draw a straight line up to the blowing edge. Do not forget the painter's tape!

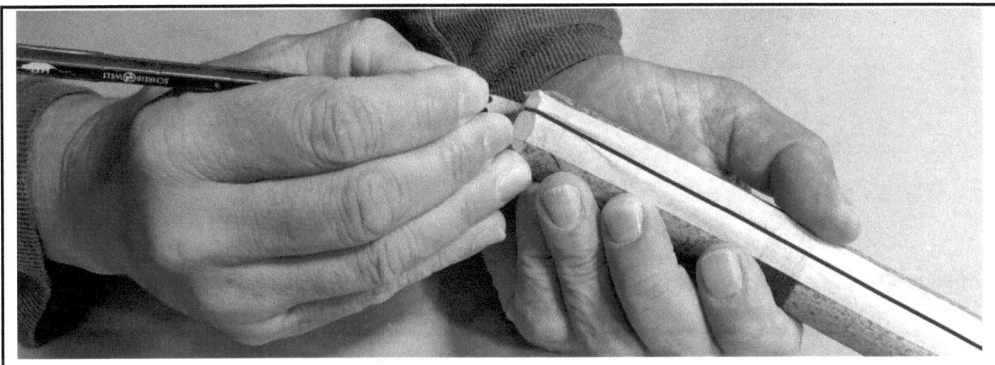

Figure 142: Fold the painter's tape over the blowing edge and stick it 1 cm (0.2 in) inside the flute.

Figure 143: Now draw a short line on the opposite side.

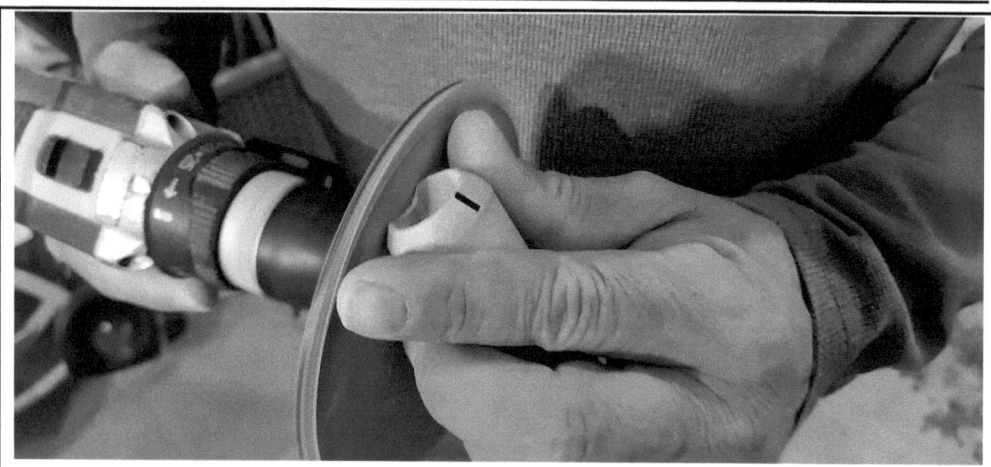

Figure 144: I shape the notch after removing the painter's tape. The small opposite line indicates the exact bottom side of the flute. I use it to drill the notch along the same axis as the finger holes. I cannot tell you how many times I placed the notch incorrectly before discovering this simple method! Yes, I lightly touch the sandpaper with my thumb and forefinger while grinding. It helps keep the flute in position and allows me to feel if I am sanding evenly. If I do not apply pressure with my fingers, I will not injure myself. However, as a beginner, you should be very cautious and consider wearing gloves, although this means you will have to rely more on sight since you will not get much tactile feedback.

Figure 145: This is how the notch looks after sanding. We still need to refine it further. Perhaps you can see the ultra-thin layer?

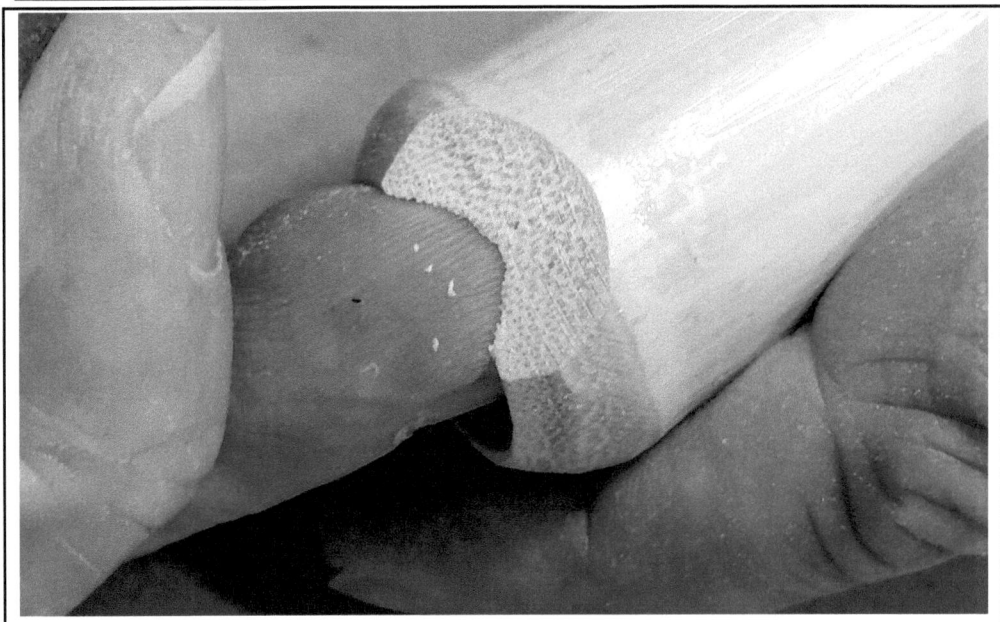

Figure 146: You can easily press out the ultra-thin layer mentioned in the previous image with a finger.

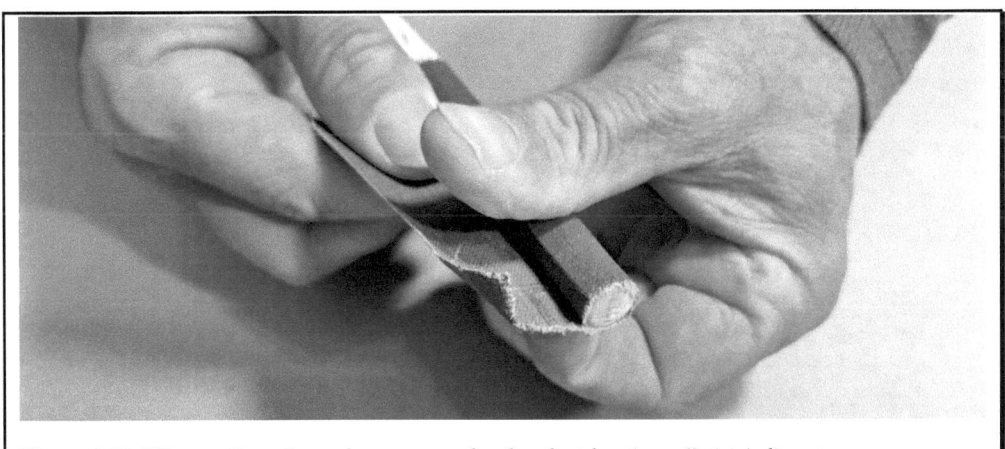

Figure 147: Wrap a fine-grit sandpaper around a dowel with a 1 cm (0.4 in) diameter.

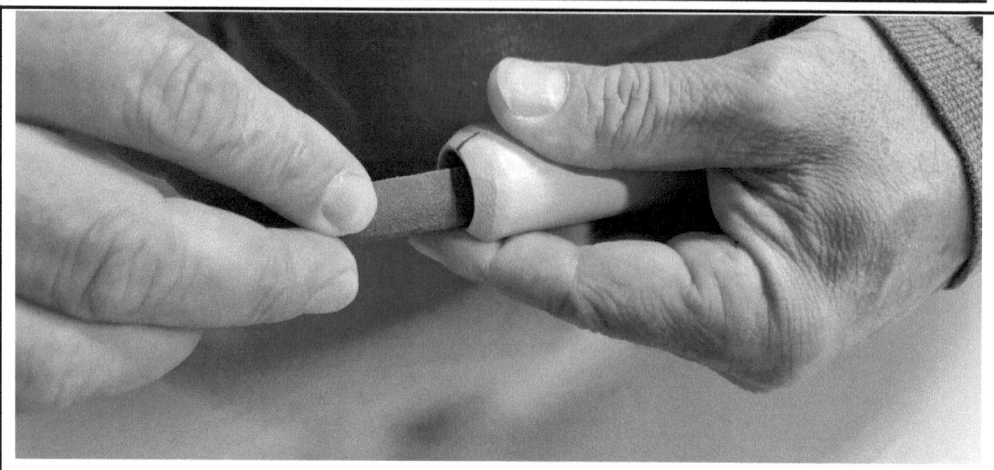

Figure 148: I sand with the sandpaper-wrapped dowel until the notch is just right. Notice how I use my left index finger to check the progress of the sanding and the notch tactilely. Be cautious with this method, and remember it is not necessary to proceed this way. After more than four decades of bamboo flute making, I have developed these habits that I cannot shake off in my old age. Also, note that the small line on the opposite side is still there, which I use for visual reference.

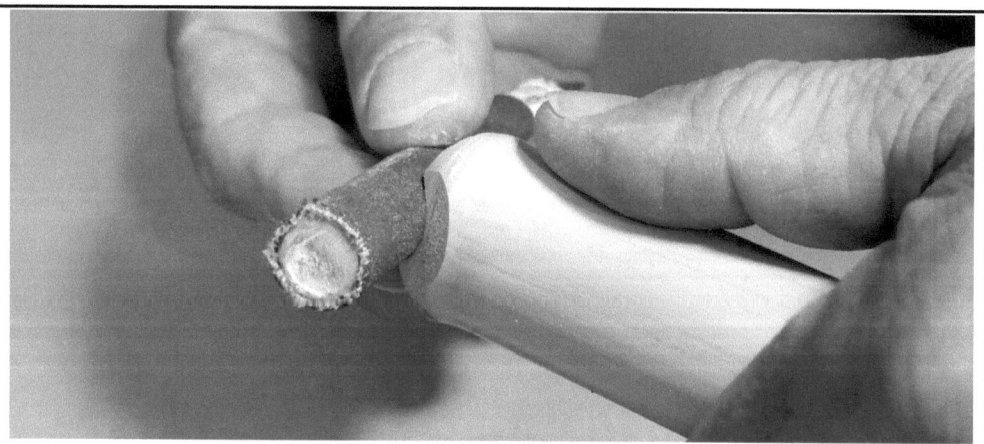

Figure 149: Last but not least, I use the same sandpaper-wrapped dowel to check if I have sanded the notch to a depth of half a centimeter (0.2 inches). I am not sanding in the picture, which would dull the notch.

The Ney Flute

I have thought quite a bit about whether to include the construction and playing method of the Ney in this book. There are many arguments in favor of doing so:

1. The tone production on the Ney is the same as on the Kawala. Therefore, any Ney player can produce a clear tone on a Kawala and vice versa.
2. The Ney was played in Egypt thousands of years ago. It is documented on the tomb reliefs of the Old Kingdom around 2700 BCE.
3. The Ney is made from the same material as the Kawala. In this book, we use bamboo, while reed (Arundo Donax) is used in the Orient.
4. The preparation of the tube, drilling of the holes, internal treatment, binding, and external treatment are all identical in making a Kawala.
5. The astonishing similarity between the Ney and the BCF also compels us to include the Ney.
6. Last but not least, it is my first instrument and that of my ancestors, who played the Ney thousands of years ago in the same place before me.

The Ney does have some unique features, some of which I mentioned in the introduction:

1. While the Kawala covers up to 2 octaves, the Ney can play three or more.
2. The Ney is tuned to the oriental quarter tone scale, unfamiliar to Western music.
3. The membranes in the Ney are not entirely removed and sanded down; the last one near the mouthpiece is largely left intact.

Since we already know how to tune a Kawala perfectly, I have decided to focus on the construction and hole-calculation method, followed by the theory and playing techniques using two scales in the Ney section of this book.

Construction of the Ney

We will build a Ney Bussilik together. There are seven Egyptian Ney sizes, all built with the same proportions. I chose the Bussilik because it is 54 cm long, making it an easy learning instrument for both men and women. The largest Egyptian Ney is 68 cm (though there are atypically larger ones), and the smallest is 37.5 cm.

Cutting the Bamboo Tube

While a Kawala can be cut at any point along the bamboo, the Ney must be cut about 5 cm above a membrane at the mouthpiece.

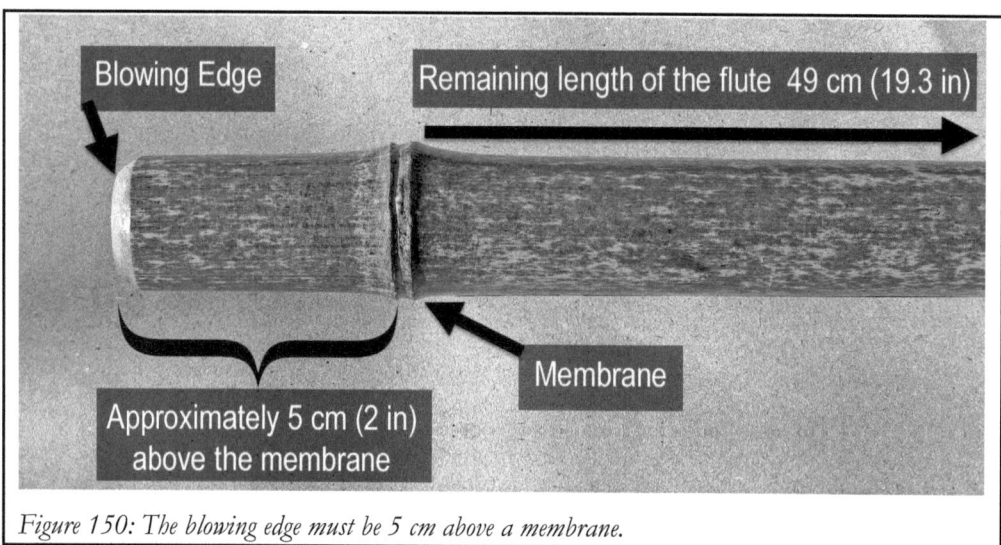

Figure 150: The blowing edge must be 5 cm above a membrane.

After cutting 5 cm above the membrane, measure 54 cm from the blowing edge, apply painter's tape at the point where you want to mark the end of the flute and cut the tube to 54 cm. If the tube is conical, ensure the wider inner diameter is at the blowing edge. The inner diameter of the tube should be about 18-20 mm (0.70-0.78 in).

Neys are mostly made from reed, although they can also be made from bamboo, which is less common. This preference is not due to the properties of reeds but because in Egypt, the birthplace of the Ney about 5,000 years ago, only reeds grew. Certainly, in Egypt, I also made them from reed. However, for the past two decades, I have been crafting them from bamboo because it actually has better properties for the Ney than the reed. For instance, sanding the inside of a reed is always problematic because it is thin and can break easily. This is less likely to happen with bamboo.

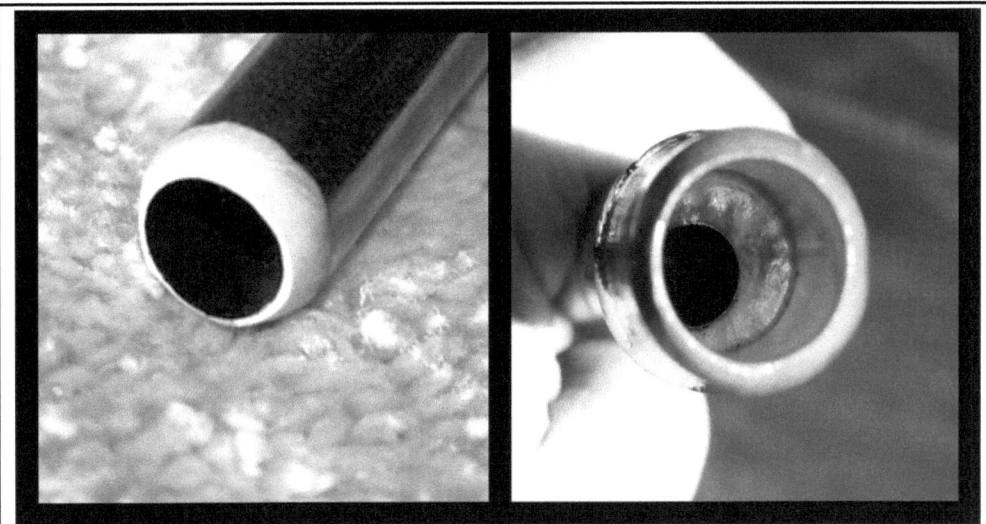

Figure 151: **Left:** *Sanded down like a Kawala.* **Right:** *The membrane approximately 5 cm (2 in) behind the blowing edge must not be filed away entirely! All other membranes must be sanded off.*

Look at the picture on the right. You can see that the Ney has a significant distinction.

The membrane about 5 cm (2 in) behind the blowing edge must not be sanded away. Instead, it has a round hole about 1 cm (0.4 in) in diameter, which I create as follows:

1. I drill a 7 mm (0.28 in) hole in the membrane using a drill.

2. Then, I use a 10 mm (0.4 in) burning rod, at least 6 cm (2.36 in) long, to enlarge the hole from 7 mm (0.28 in) to 10 mm (0.4 in). While doing this, I constantly rotate the Ney along its longitudinal axis to prevent the hole from becoming oval, although an oval shape would not cause any harm. This process only takes a few seconds. If the burning rod remains in the membrane for too long, it can burn away completely. In that case, the tube can no longer be used for a Ney.

3. All other membranes in the flute body must be sanded entirely away!

Calculating and Drilling the Holes

Calculating the hole positions for the Ney is more challenging than for the Kawala. You must fully understand the calculation system before you begin building a Ney.

Practice drawing it on a piece of paper until you have it memorized!

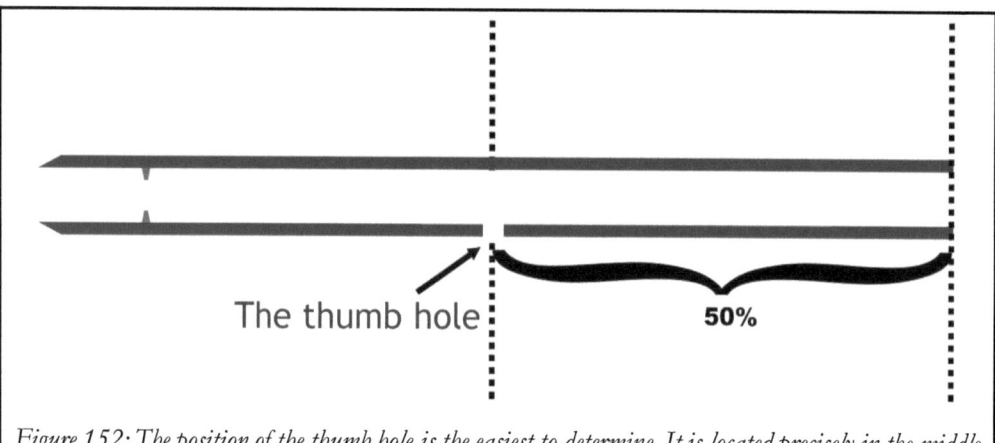

The thumb hole

50%

Figure 152: The position of the thumb hole is the easiest to determine. It is located precisely in the middle of the flute. Mark its position, but drill the thumb hole last. You will soon understand why.

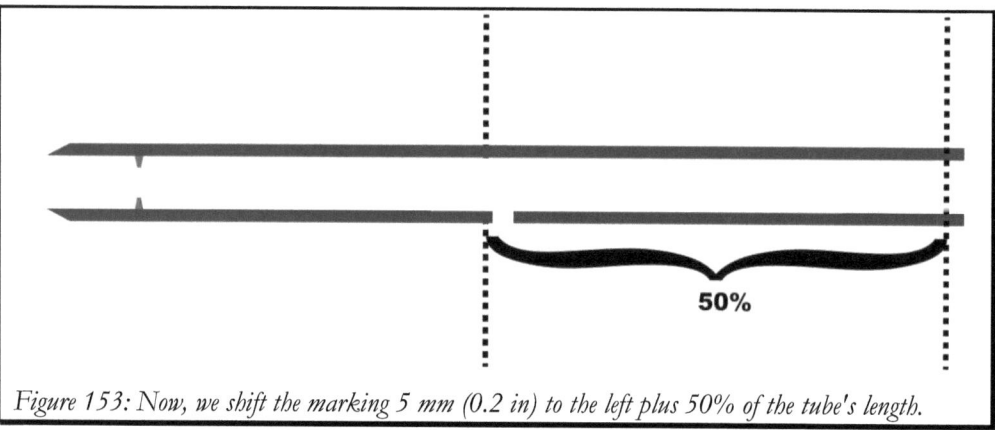

50%

Figure 153: Now, we shift the marking 5 mm (0.2 in) to the left plus 50% of the tube's length.

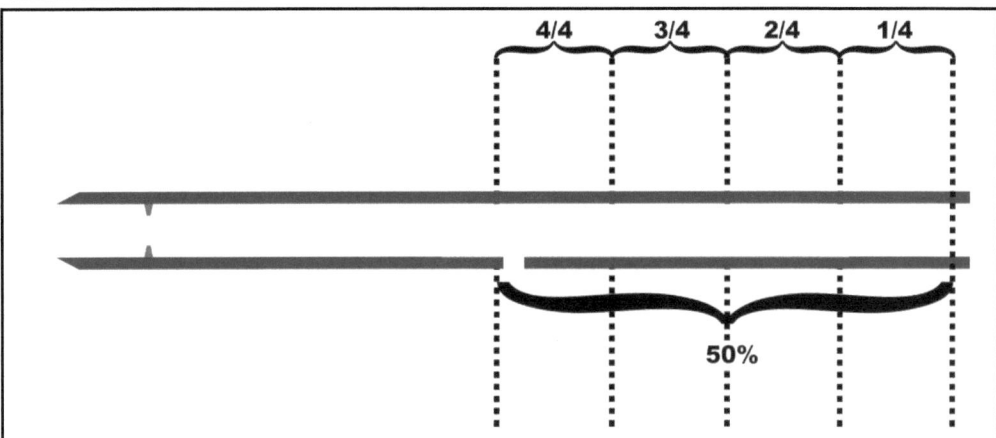

Figure 154: In the next step, we divide these 50% into four equal sections (each 12.5% of the entire flute), which I refer to here as 1/4 to 4/4, starting from the bottom to the middle.

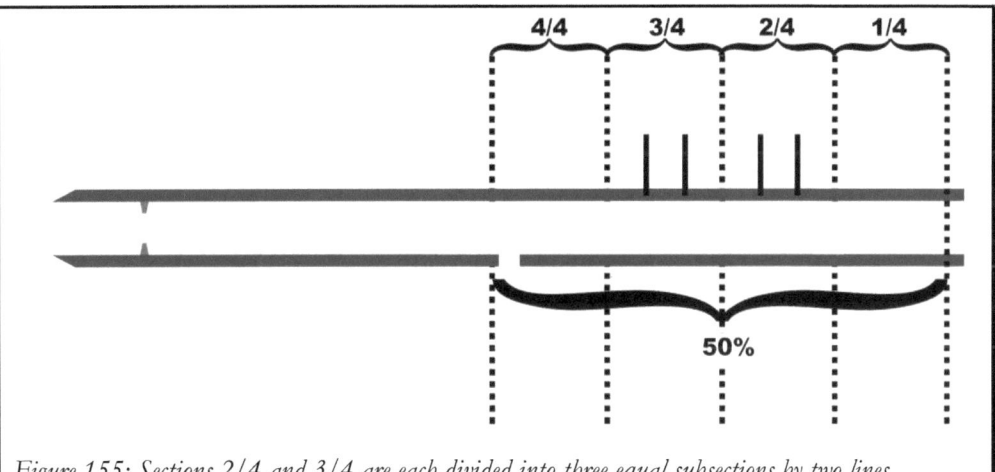

Figure 155: Sections 2/4 and 3/4 are each divided into three equal subsections by two lines.

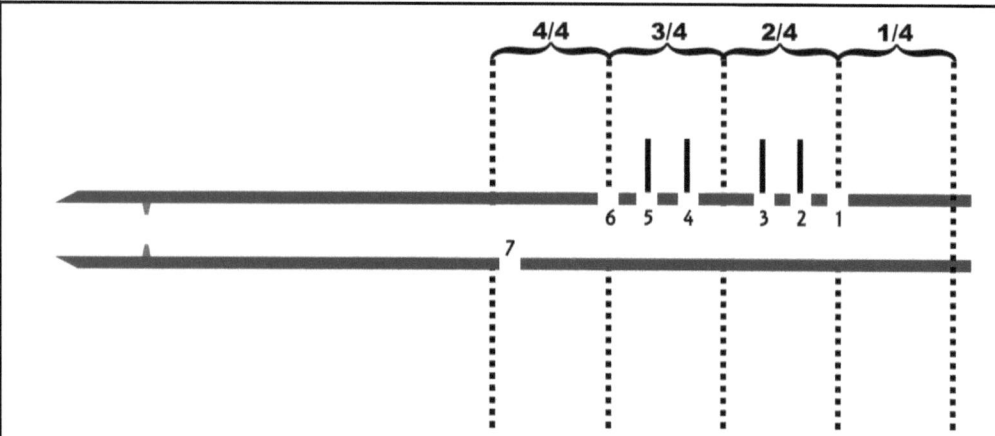

Figure 156: Now you have calculated the positions for your holes. Hole (1) is precisely on the line that divides 1/4 of section 2/4. Next are holes (2) and (3) at the positions of the subsections. Then, skip one marking, the line between 2/4 and 3/4, to drill holes (4), (5), and (6). Hole (7) must be drilled precisely on the opposite side of the flute at 50% of the flute's length.

Hole Position Secret and Own Ney Sizes

If you reflect for a second on this hole system, you will find that it is not so different from the Kwala hole system, where we divided the length by 12. Here, we divide the quarters 2/4 and 3/4 into three sections. If we would do this throughout the flute, we would have 4x3 sections in the lower half and imaginary 4x3 sections in the upper half. Essentially, we have the length divided by 24. The reason for that is that in oriental music, we have between each half step the quarter tones, hence factually 24 notes in an octave.

Having understood all this so far allows us to use a percentage table to calculate the hole positions. All you need to do is have the proper diameter and proper length. However, knowing the hole position secret allows you to be creative and design other Ney flutes with any desirable fundamental note. The table on the right side reveals these positions for you. Remember that we always start counting the holes from the bottom of the flute towards the blowing edge.

Hole	Position
H1	13.00 %
H2	17.17 %
H3	21.33 %
H4	29.67 %
H5	33.83 %
H6	38.00 %
H7 (thumb)	50.00 %

The Problem with the Thumb Hole

A common problem when drilling thumb holes is that they are often mismarked. They are frequently not aligned with the line below the upper holes and are drilled slightly off-center, even though they are the correct distance from the blowing edge regarding the length of the flute. Such errors result in an improper grip on the Ney, leading to instability while playing.

I solve this problem as follows. After drilling the upper holes, I rotate the flute and press it diagonally against the edge of a table so that one of the upper holes is aligned with the table edge.

I then draw a line along what appears to be the topmost side, which is the opposite of the already drilled holes. I drill the thumb hole where this line intersects with the marking for the hole (7).

The following images illustrate this process in more detail:

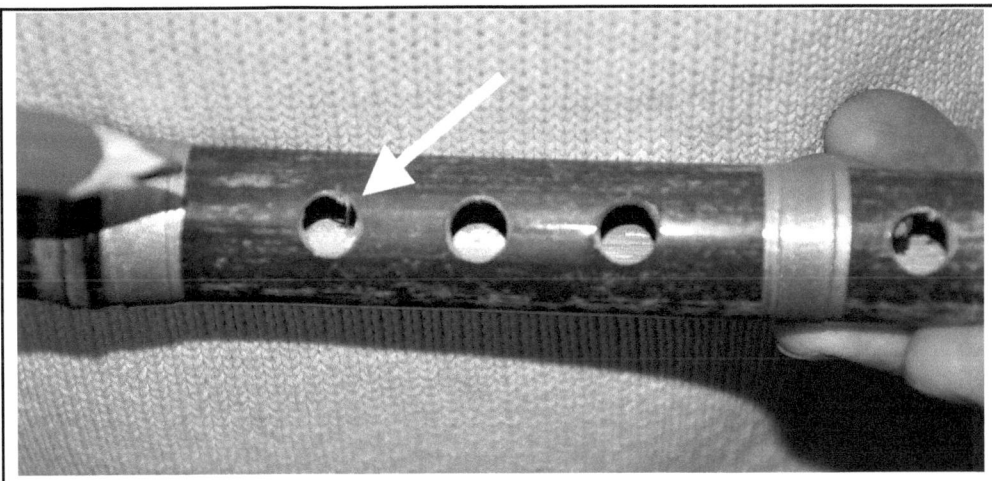

Figure 157: These are the top three holes of a Ney, where I had not yet tuned the holes. The white arrow points to the sixth hole, as we will refer to it in two images.

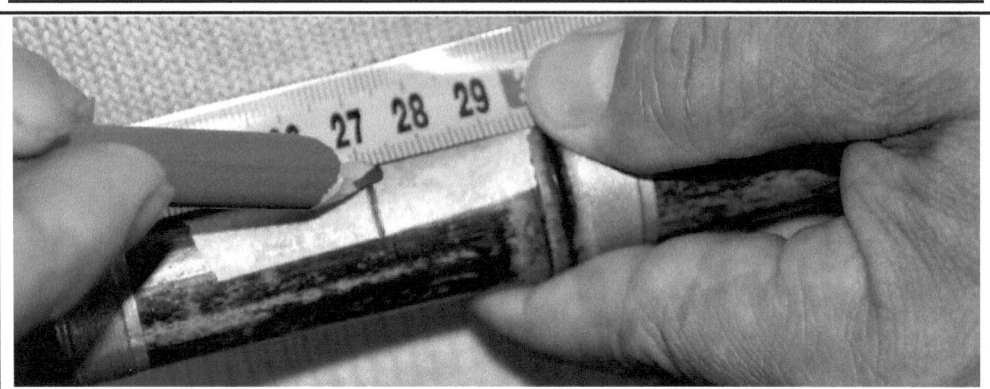

Figure 158: I turn the flute by eye to draw a line along the center of the flute on the opposite side of the finger holes at approximately 27 cm from the mouthpiece.

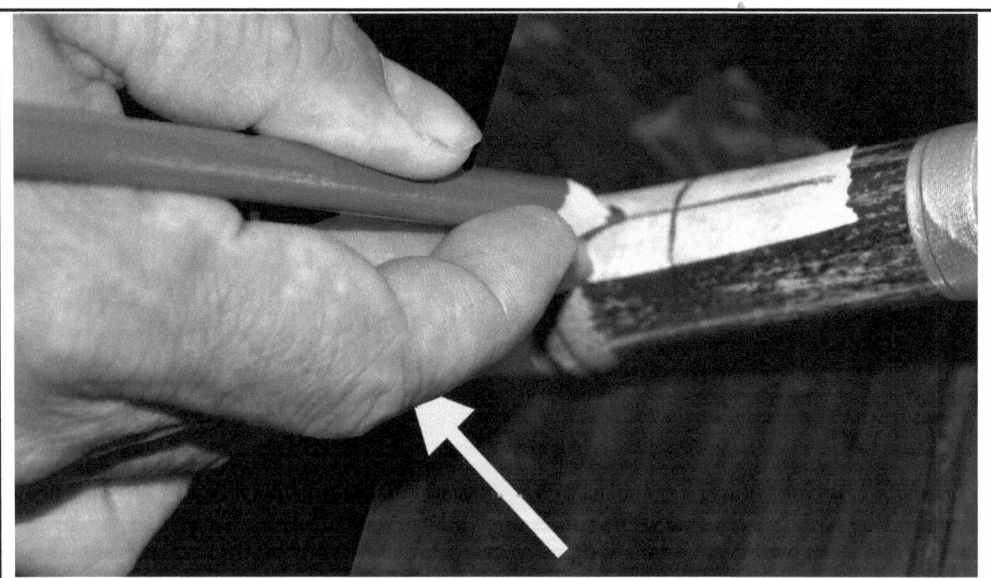

Figure 159: I press the flute against the edge of a table so that hole (6) fits snugly against the table edge, with the foot of the flute pressed against my belly and the top pressed with my left hand. Then, I draw a vertical line with my right hand that intersects with the previous line (center of the flute) to find the position of the thumb hole.

As with the Kawala, using a drill bit with a smaller diameter is essential. An 8 mm (0.31 in) drill bit is ideal. The holes are burned to the necessary size of 9-11 mm (0.35-0.43 in), just as I explained with the Kawala. It would be best if you only began fine-tuning your Ney once you have understood the theory.

You may have noticed in Figure 156 that my holes were significantly larger than 8 mm (0.31 in). After making a few hundred flutes, you intuitively enlarge the holes in the correct position.

Theory of the Ney Flute

In the major scale for the Kawala, we used the formula 0-2-2-1-2-2-2-1. These intervals correspond to half steps. As a reminder, using a piano keyboard, we determined that there are 12 notes in an octave in Western music, from one C to the next C. To calculate the major scales, we used a practical chart where we placed our formula **0-2-2-1-2-2-2-1** under the respective notes.

However, the Ney is a musical instrument from a different tradition. We discussed above that instead of just 12 notes in Western music, the Oriental music knows 24 notes in an octave because we have these quarter tones.

In the Western chromatic scale, you would have the following case from C to D:

C	C#	D
0	Half	Whole

In an Oriental quarter-tone scale has the following notes between C and D:

C	C‡	C#	D♭	D
0	Quarter sharp	Half	Quarter flat	Whole

Of course, the D♭ can be understood as a quarter tone below the D and three-quarter tones above the C.

No matter what Ney size you want to build, the holes of the Ney always have the following tonal distances from each other, starting from the lowest note (all holes closed), which we call here zero:

Zero – Whole – Half – Quarter – Three quarters – Half – Half – Whole

Or the formula: $0 – 4/4 – 2/4 – 1/4 – 3/4 – 2/4 – 2/4 – 4/4$

The following figure illustrates this relationship using a Ney:

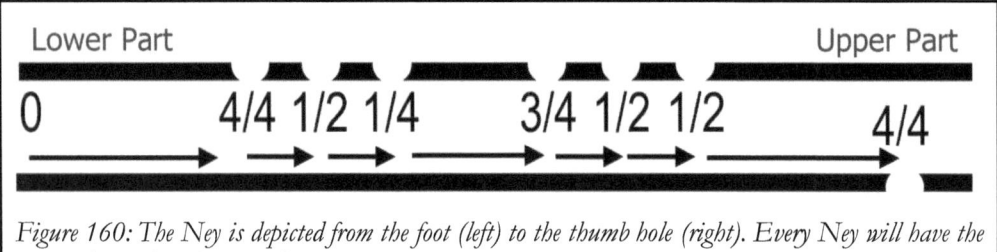

Figure 160: The Ney is depicted from the foot (left) to the thumb hole (right). Every Ney will have the same relationships between the notes.

However, it is not customary to consider the base note (0) as the root note of the scale on the Ney. Instead, the root is the note produced when the first hole is opened. For example, the **Bussilik** is tuned to E, so the lowest note (base note), when all holes are closed, is not an E but a D. This is surely important for playing the Ney, but for building the flute, we simply take the base note as the start of our calculation.

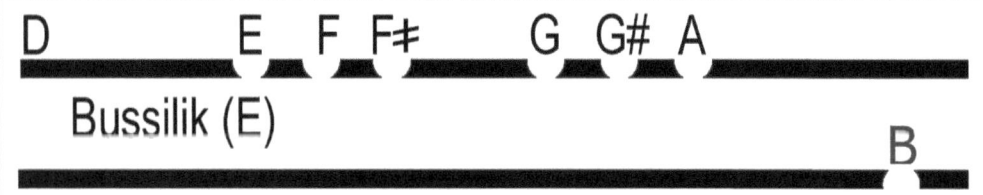

Figure 161: If you apply the above formula to a Ney tuned to E, the lowest note will be a D. Note that the quarter tone comes from the third hole. This is true for all Neys, as long as the root note and hole positions are correct.

Copy-Table for Ney Flute Calculation

C	C𝄲	C#	D𝄳	D	D𝄲	D#	E𝄳
E	F𝄳	F	F𝄲	F#	G𝄳	G	G𝄲
G#	A𝄳	A	A𝄲	A#	B𝄳	B	B𝄲
C	C𝄲	C#	D𝄳	D	D𝄲	D#	E𝄳
E	F𝄳	F	F𝄲	F#	G𝄳	G	G𝄲
G#	A𝄳	A	A𝄲	A#	B𝄳	B	B𝄲

Feel free to copy this table, which includes two octaves and quarter tones. You can use it to calculate your Ney. Take the calculation formula from the previous page, and you can build any Ney, regardless of the base note you have chosen for your reed.

As a Ney maker, you should know that there are seven standard Egyptian Ney sizes. Traditionally, people would make an additional seven Neys tuned a half note higher and another seven Neys slightly lower pitch. It allowed musicians to play almost any piece of music. Each pitch has a specific name, which you should memorize as a Ney player and a Ney maker. All the Ney sizes I mention here are based on bamboo tubes with an internal diameter of 18-20 mm (0.70-0.78 in), although the shorter flutes have slightly smaller diameters and finger holes.

1. Ney Rast (C), approximately 68.00 cm (26.8 in) long
2. Ney Doka (D), approximately 60.00 cm (23.60 in) long
3. Ney Bussilik (E), approximately 54.00 cm (21.25 in) long
4. Ney Djaharka (F), approximately 51.00 cm (20.10 in)long
5. Ney Nawa (G), approximately 44.50 cm (17.50 in) long
6. Ney Husseini (A), approximately 40.50 cm (15.95 in) long
7. Ney Adjam (B), approximately 37.50 cm (14.75) long

In Turkish music, there are even larger Neys, up to 97 cm (3.18 ft). Since you know the secret of the finger holes, you can theoretically make any size if you can still play it comfortably.

Let us assume you want to build a Ney in Eb. Then you should cut it to a length of about 57 cm (22.45 in) because your target Ney lies between the Doka (D) and Bussilik (E). Here is the calculation in cm: (60+54)/2=57 cm. For those using inches, it would be: (23.60+21.25)/2=22.43 in].

I recommend initially cutting it to 58 cm (22.85 in), preparing the blowing edge and the first membrane, and then sanding down the rest of the tube while continuously testing if the base note is one note below the Eb, which would be a clean Db. Once you achieve this, you just need to calculate and mark the positions of the holes, as previously explained. Afterward, you should insert the formula into a copy of the table provided above to check and tune the note of your Ney finger holes. (Remember: **0 – 4/4 – 2/4 – 1/4 – 3/4 – 2/4 – 2/4 – 4/4**)

For practice, I will calculate the expected notes in a Ney Eb for you on the next page. I strongly recommend you try it independently and then check the results with my calculation.

C	C‡	C#	D♭	D	D‡	D#	E♭
		0				4/4	

E	F♭	F	F‡	F#	G♭	G	G‡
2/4	1/4			3/4		2/4	

G#	A♭	A	A‡	A#	B♭	B	B‡
2/4				4/4			

Now you know which note should be produced by each corresponding hole. Therefore, you can start drilling the holes. As you learned with the Kawala, begin with the first hole (counting from the bottom of the flute) and test it immediately before drilling the next hole.

But be careful!

Although the first hole should produce an E, it might produce a Bb (A#). This is not necessarily incorrect! The Ney is played across four registers, depending on how sharp you blow the edge. I will be explaining this below. At this stage, we need to know that the first register is merely a bass copy of the second register. But the third register produces note B from the first hole, and the fourth returns to produce an E.

The following table shows you the different notes produced from the first hole on the different registers:

The first hole on four registers using a Ney Bussilik

Register	Hole 1	Base note
1st Register	E	D
2nd Register	E	D
3rd Register	B	A
4th Register	E	D
5th Register	/	F♯

I have been talking about four registers but wrote a fifth one here. This fifth register is hard to play and must be enormously overblown, causing a noticeable sharp tuning on this register. Hence, I only added the F♯ for the fifth register, which can be reached on the fourth register when opening hole Nr. 3. This might sound complicated now, but it will become easier in two or three graphics. Sometimes, you need to complete the entire circle to find the center. Please be patient.

The Ney is not a Kawala, even if we produce the sound exactly the same way. With the Kawala, it does not matter whether you play the first or second register; the notes are always the same, just an octave apart. The holes on the Kawala extend over half of the flute, explicitly taking up 7/12 of its length.

With the Ney, however, things are different. The holes are positioned in the second and third eighths of the flute (counting from the bottom). The thumb hole serves only to connect the first register with the second (more on this below).

While the holes on the Kawala form a scale by simply opening the finger holes in sequence, this is not the case with the Ney. On the Ney, the beginning and end of a scale depend on the specific fingering you choose to play. Consequently, a single Ney can be used to play multiple scales.

The following page is a graphic showing all the standard notes that the Bussilik Ney allows you to play.

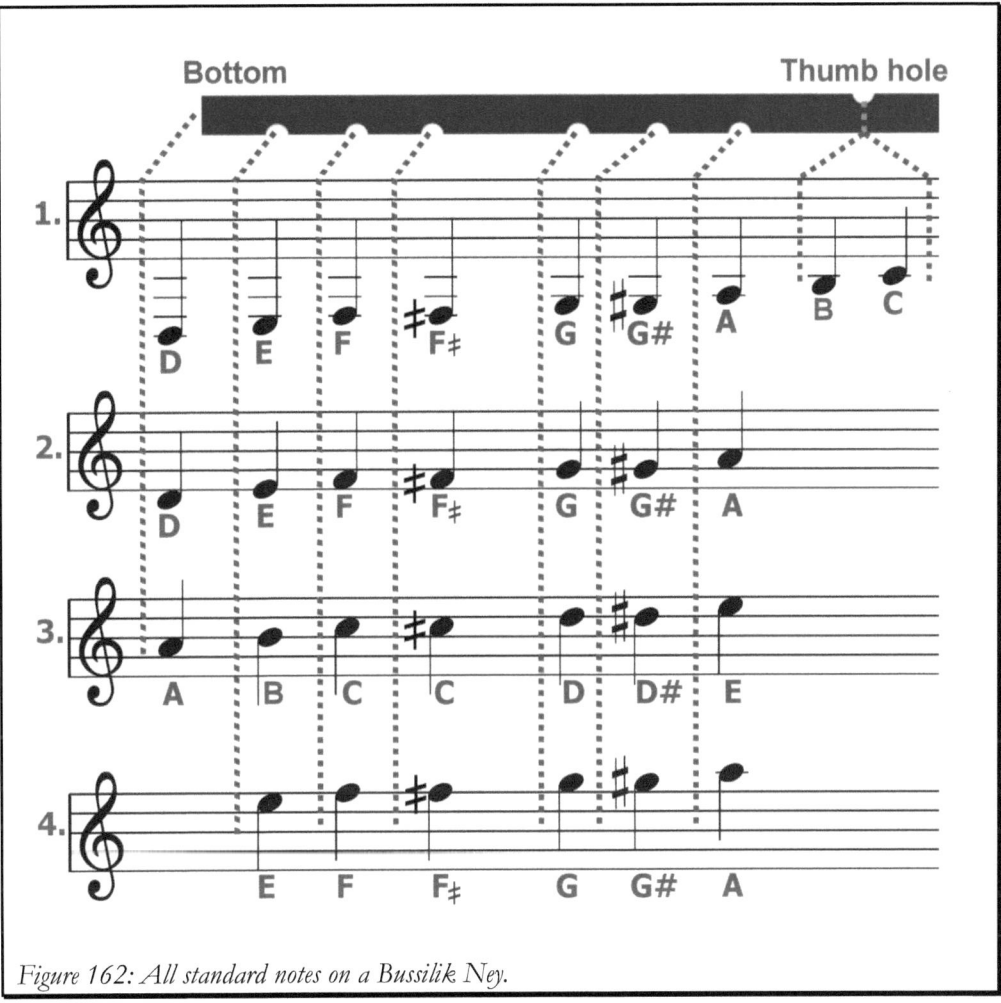

Figure 162: All standard notes on a Bussilik Ney.

Additionally, several intermediary notes can be produced by half-closing the holes.

You should be able to observe the following:

1. The thumb hole is generally played only in the first register. It is used by opening it a quarter, half, three-quarters, or entirely, allowing you to

produce all notes between A and D. In the graphic, I have included only two notes as examples.

2. Since the second register also begins with D, you can connect the scales between the first and second registers using the thumb hole.

3. The sixth hole in the second register produces an A, identical to the A of the first hole in the third register. Therefore, the B♭ (A#) needed for a scale is played by half-closing the first hole in the third register. Theoretically, you could achieve this with the thumb hole in the second register.

4. The sixth hole in the third register produces an E, which is identical to the second hole in the fourth register. In most scales, you play the E in the third register and start the fourth register at F or F#

Once you have played the Ney for a while, you likely will not focus on these details anymore, as the Ney is almost always played by ear. However, for tuning a Ney, these theoretical insights are essential! Try to blow into the second register when tuning your Ney, as it provides the best pitch for tuning.

Always remember: the note of the first hole in the third register equals that of the sixth hole in the second register. So, if you play an A instead of an E, do not be alarmed; you might be in the third register.

Everything you learned about fine-tuning with the Kawala can be applied here directly. Afterward, you can treat it from the inside and outside, just like a Kawala.

When a Ney player favors the Saba scale, they will play it when acquiring a Ney and immediately notice if something is wrong.

Since different scales require different finger holes to be skipped or covered, we will learn the Saba scale and the Rast scale, which will allow us to use the finger holes that are not used in the Saba scale.

But first, we should briefly discuss the progression of the registers, as you do not start each register by closing all the holes.

Climbing the Registers of a Ney

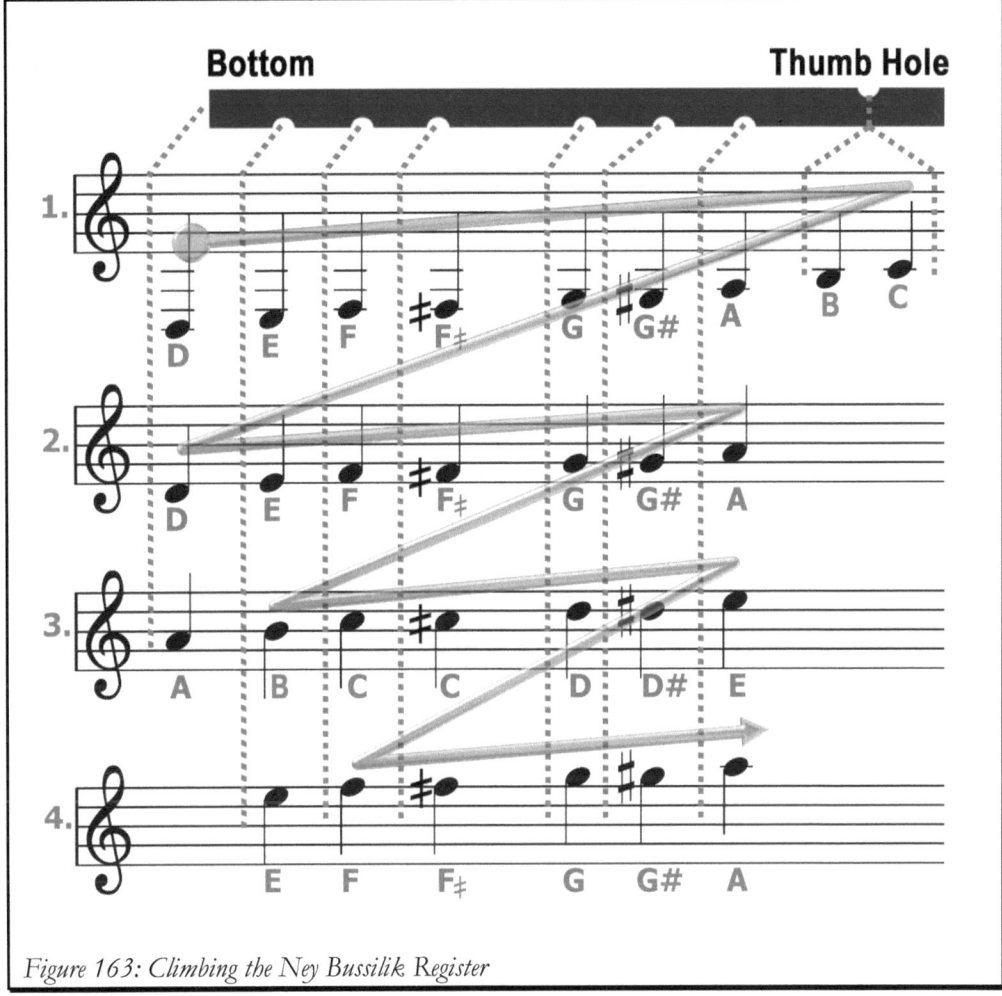

Figure 163: Climbing the Ney Bussilik Register

Please follow the grey line in Figure 161. Notice that you have an A when opening all finger holes but the thumb in the first register. If you open the thumb hole entirely, you will jump from an A to a C. Hence, you half-close to get a B. Then you start the second register with all holes closed, the third with the lowest hole already opened, and the fourth with the first and second holes from the bottom open. It will not sound like a scale, but you will notice how the pitch increases each time. After training this full range of notes on a Ney, move on to learn the Rast and Saba scales on the Ney.

The Rast Scale on a Bussilik (E)

The Rast scale is very popular because of its simplicity. The scale is not limited to the 68 cm Ney, also called Rast. The Rast Ney is one thing, but the Rast scale can be played on any Ney. The intervals between the notes are as follows:

Whole - Three quarters - Three quarters - Whole - Whole - Three quarters - Three quarters.

As a formula, this is: $0 - 4/4 - 3/4 - 3/4 - 4/4 - 4/4 - 3/4 - 3/4$

Although the Bussilik is understood as a Ney in E, the Rast scale is best played from D.

C	C‡	C#	D♭	D	D‡	D#	E♭
				0			
E	F♭	F	F‡	F#	G♭	G	G‡
4/4			3/4			3/4	
G#	A♭	A	A‡	A#	B♭	B	B‡
		4/4				4/4	
C	C‡	C#	D♭	D	D‡	D#	E♭
	3/4			3/4			

Figure 164: Calculating the Rast Scale on D. All the required notes can be found on a Bussilik Ney.

Fingering Chart for the Rast Scale

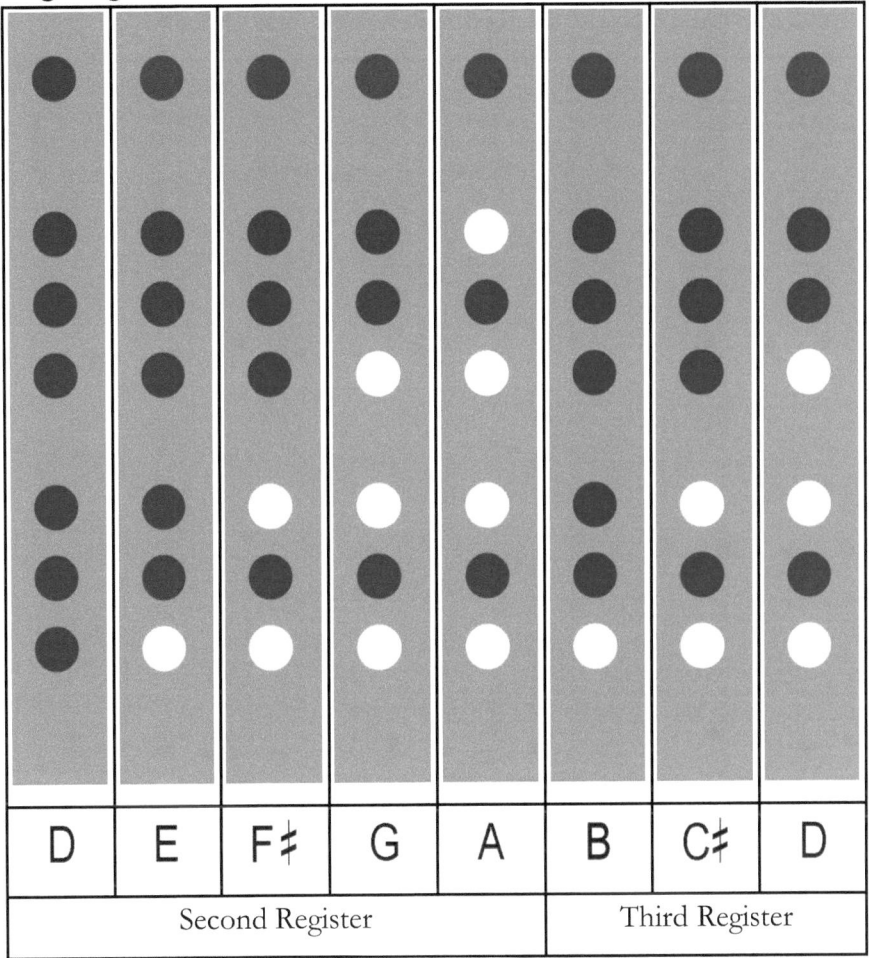

D	E	F♯	G	A	B	C♯	D

| Second Register | | | | Third Register | | | |

Notice that I always have the second hole closed in the F, G, A, C, and last D. This is actually not necessary to influence the tone but helps you control the grip on the flute. This Rast scale fingering chart you have just seen works for any Ney, regardless of how high or low it is tuned, as long as the hole proportions are correct. This means that if you play a Rast scale on a Ney Doka, you will automatically start your Rast scale on a whole note below the Doka (D). Hence, your Rast scale with a Doka Ney will be on C.

Rast Scale Exercise: Silent Walk

Here is a small exercise piece for the Rast scale on the Ney Bussilik:

Figure 165: Silent Walk (M. Hassan). After the repeat sign, you move through the C and B of the thumb hole into the first register.

"Khissara" A Musical Piece in Rast for the Bussilik Ney

I have named the piece "Khissara" (Loss or Sorrow). A typical feature of Ney music is its melancholy; even the happiest Ney pieces always reveal a touch of melancholy, and this one is no exception.

Figure 166: Khissara (Rast) - M. Hassan

Both musical pieces are written focusing on the second and third registers. One should always practice the Arabic scales on these two levels. Scales must be practiced and played until you can hum them effortlessly. The key issue is not where you start but whether you recognize the relationships between the notes. Once you have mastered the Rast on the second and third registers, you will find that you can intuitively play the scale on the low first and high fourth registers.

The Saba Scale on a Bussilik (E)

The Saba scale is particularly popular and well-known to many people. If you play the Saba as a European in an oriental country, people will be amazed and love you! Saba is engrained in the oriental culture, and the term is used synonymously for melancholic moods.

The relationships between the notes are as follows:

Three quarters - Three quarters - Half - Six quarters - Half - Whole - Whole

In formula form, this is: $0 - 3/4 - 3/4 - 2/4 - 6/4 - 2/4 - 4/4 - 4/4$

E	F♭	F	F‡	F#	G♭	G	G‡
0			3/4			3/4	
G#	**A♭**	**A**	**A‡**	**A#**	**B♭**	**B**	**B‡**
2/4						6/4	
C	**C‡**	**C#**	**D♭**	**D**	**D‡**	**D#**	**E♭**
2/4				4/4			
E	**F♭**	**F**	**F‡**	**F#**	**G♭**	**G**	**G‡**
4/4							

Figure 167: Calculating the Saba Scale on D. All the required notes can be found on a Bussilik Ney

To play the Saba scale on a Ney without complicated fingerings, start with the fundamental tone of the flute (first hole open). On the Bussilik, this is the E.

Fingering Chart for the Saba Scale

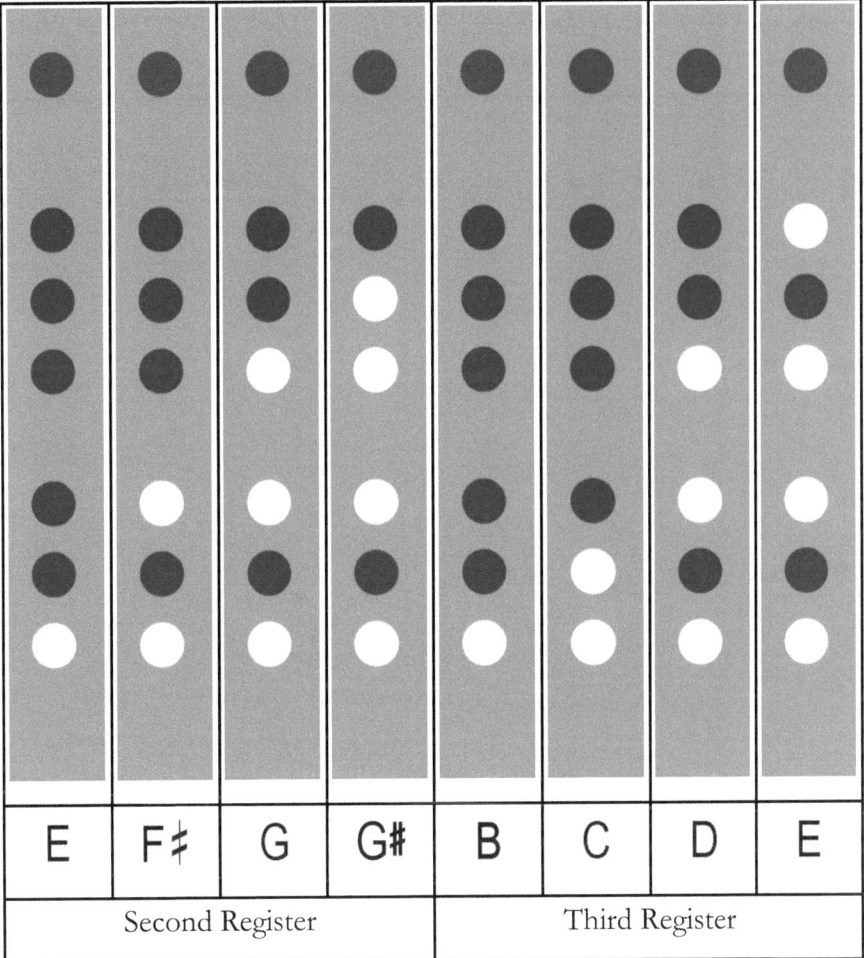

E	F♯	G	G♯	B	C	D	E
Second Register				Third Register			

Of course, this fingering chart works with any Ney. On the Ney Rast, you will have your Saba scale on C, the Ney Doka on D, the Ney Bussilik on E, and so on.

Saba Scale Exercise: Qalbi

The Saba scale on Bussilik (E) requires an F#, a G, and a G#, among other notes. To avoid confusion, the G# is written as Ab.

Figure 168: Qalbi (M. Hassan). In the last line, you move from the D (second register) through the C and B (using the thumb hole) into the first register

"Saba ya Sabaya" A Ahort Saba Piece for the Bussilik Ney

Figure 169: Saba Ya Sabaya

Perhaps a final word on Ney flutes. In the West here, there is a strong focus on playing the notes exactly as they are written. In Egypt, where I started playing Ney some 48 years ago, most Ney players used to play by ear. Their playing together with other musicians relied mainly on experience and mutual listening. This does not mean you distort the melody entirely, but you are expected to move freely with the Ney, adding nuances like singers with their voices. So, do not take the notes above too seriously. Consider them as a guideline for a melody, and try to play them in a way that pleases you. In the YouTube era, you can find countless pieces in Saba and Rast and just play along.

Finally

This is my fourth book on rim-blown flutes; the first three are in German. In 2012, I wrote a German Book, which can be translated into "Kawala & Ney: The Eldest Instruments of Humanity."

I had been planning to translate this book since I wrote it, but as the years passed by, raising children, working, and re-studying, I never had the time. When I finally started to translate the book, I decided to expand it. Not only have I learned more over the last 12 years, but I also wanted to add the Saluang and Pueblo flutes. Sure, there are many other rim-blown flutes that I build and could add in here, but I deliberately took you into all the details of discovering how to tune the Puebloan Broken Cave Flutes so that you can go on and measure, calculate, and rebuild any flute.

For instance, try to search for the Puebloan Hopi flute and rebuild it. You have one in the Museum of Fine Arts, Boston's collection here:

https://collections.mfa.org/objects/50798.

If you wish to hear one of mine, use the QR code on the right side. Though I explained it in German, I also demonstrated how to play it.

Figure 170: Puebloan Hopi Flute

I am infinitely grateful to have been blessed with an interest in bamboo flutes at a very young age. It has accompanied me throughout my life and given me more than I could mention. My goal has always been to connect cultures through my flutes. I have played my flutes on different markets, at feasts, with the Berlin Philharmonic, Gregorian choir singers, and gospel choirs. My flutes are played in film productions, major musicals, and even military orchestras, but one event touched me deeply. When I was in Frankfurt am Main (Germany), I heard young street musicians with the sound of a bamboo flute familiar to me. I went up to them, and the flute player recognized me from some online tutorials and approached me. He proudly showed me the flute he had built after studying my books. That was the moment I knew I had begun to achieve my goal of connecting cultures. I am very grateful for this, and I hope this English book will further contribute to that goal.

Good luck with building and playing all the flutes in this book. And who knows, you might even start a business with building flutes, as some have in Germany after studying my German books. But remember: you can learn everything, but experience must be gained. Therefore, I advise you to build many, very many flutes. Intuition in building, unique new ideas, and solutions for obstacles are things you must experience and discover yourself, and you will be able to do so.

Eberswalde (Germany) 05.08.2024

Your Notes